CONCILIUM
Religion in the Seventies

CONCILIUM

EDITORIAL DIRECTORS:
BASIC EDITORIAL COMMITTEES: Roland Murphy and Bruce Vawter (Scripture) • Giuseppe Alberigo and Anton Weiler (Church History)

EDITORIAL COMMITTEES: *Group I: Christian Faith:* Edward Schillebeeckx and Bas van Iersel (Dogma) • Hans Küng and Walter Kasper (Ecumenism) • Johann Baptist Metz and Jean-Pierre Jossua (Fundamental Theology) *Group II: Christian Ethics:* Franz Böckle and Jacques-Marie Pohier (Moral Theology) • Christian Duquoc and Casiano Floristán (Spirituality) • Andrew Greeley and Gregory Baum (Sociology of Religion) *Group III: The Practical Church:* Alois Müller and Norbert Greinacher (Pastoral Theology) • Herman Schmidt and David Power (Liturgy) • Peter Huizing and William Bassett (Canon Law)

THEOLOGICAL ADVISERS: Juan Alfaro • Marie-Dominique Chenu • Yves Congar • Gustavo Gutiérrez Merino • René Laurentin • Karl Rahner • Roberto Tucci

LAY SPECIALIST ADVISERS: Luciano Caglioti • August-Wilhelm von Eiff • Paulo Freire • Jean Ladrière • Pedro Lain Entralgo • Paul Ricoeur • Barbara Ward Jackson • Harald Weinrich

SECRETARY: Mlle Hanny Hendriks, Arksteestraat 3–Nijme ; en, The Netherlands

New Series: Volume 5, Number 10: Fundamental Theology

THEOLOGY OF JOY

Edited by
Johann Baptist Metz and Jean-Pierre Jossua

Herder and Herder

1974
HERDER AND HERDER NEW YORK
815 Second Avenue
New York 10017

ISBN: 0-8164-2579-5

Library of Congress Catalog Card Number: 73-17903
Copyright © 1974 by Herder and Herder Inc. and Stichting Concilium

Printed in the United States

CONTENTS

Editorial

Joy and Grief, Cheerfulness, Melancholy and Humour or "the Difficulty of Saying Yes"

Note: The (real) title, "On the Difficulty of Saying Yes", applies to section III of the editorial. Before this, however, section I discusses the original idea for this issue in the context of the tasks of fundamental theology. Section II then describes the actual structure and individual topics of the issue.

I

Fundamental theology is always an attempt to put new experiences into words, to give sympathetic but critical expression to new and inarticulate moods and choices and turn them into a challenge to the life of Church and society. In this attempt to work out practical criteria for new experiences and moods, fundamental theology itself is in a special way exploratory, and makes use of hypothesis and experiment. It is not arbitrary, however, because its aim throughout is to understand the new experiences as a making present of that dangerously liberating memory of Jesus Christ by which our Christian life constantly seeks to redefine its identity and acquire a sense of direction. It is impossible to say in advance what is important and what unimportant to fundamental theology. To find out, the theologian is forced to make experiments—not for the sake of successful adaptation or blind subordination to "time", but in order to give expression in the Logos of theology (which means in the form of a story) to genuinely new experiences and not just to

7

concepts based on previous experience. He will do this "in season and out of season" (cf. 2 Tim. 4. 2), critically and self-critically.

Are not our lives falling more and more under the control of an apathetic, that is, an unfeeling rationality? Does not the modern world suffer from an inbuilt suspicion of imagination, feeling, suffering and passion? And does this not mean that our advanced societies are dominated by new taboos on mourning, melancholy and suffering? Of course the question might equally be asked from the other side—is an insistence on "moods" of this sort anything more than mere nostalgia, a regressive splitting up and paralysis of the state of consciousness we have finally reached after so much struggle? What cognitive, functional and even political significance is contained in these "pathetic" dimensions of our lives? What are the results of their suppression? And what particular form should practical responsibility for the Christian faith take in this situation, given that the Christian message emphasizes joy?

These, more or less, were the ideas behind the planning of this issue. Its contents include such topics as joy as against mourning, cheerfulness as opposed to melancholy and finally humour. We deliberately refrained from any attempt to give a precise definition of the subject we had in mind, since it would not only have very quickly reached semantic limits, but would also have encouraged either a purely systematic and *a priori* or a purely historical treatment. Rather than either of those, we wanted this issue of *Concilium* to be a sort of paradigmatic solution from which important areas of this inexhaustible field would become crystallized and in which our historical and social situation would be part of the mixture. We also hoped that this would prevent the subject from being analysed into the familiar categories. Paradigm was to take precedence over system, and the essay was to have pride of place as a form. This is why in putting this issue together we rejected in advance the familiar "bulletin" section and replaced it with a series of shortish essays. We felt that using essays offered some guarantee that the content we wanted to get into this issue (which included "humour", for example) would not be negated in advance by the form in which it was discussed.

II

The structure of the issue can perhaps best be seen if we divide the material into four sections.

A first section, based mainly on analysis and discussion of the present situation, offers "perspectives". In the first article, David Steere deals with the "inability to mourn" and the "difficulty of being happy". Past and present forms of the "melancholy of fulfilment" by means of a threefold division of sadness—the sadness of beauty, of victory and of success (Landmann). Finally, Eugen Biser suggests how Christian self-criticism can offer a way of defeating what Nietzsche called the "spirit of gravity".

The second section deals with "principles". First in this section is an attempt to use modern work in linguistic analysis to define the meaning and limitations of predicating joy and sorrow of God (Fiorenza). A second philosophical study discusses the question of humour as a theological virtue (Bessière). In the last article in this section, Jacques Colette begins with the significance of Mozart to Karl Barth and goes on to discuss the relation of theology and aesthetics in general to language. (This article was originally called "Inside the 'System': Music. Mozart in Karl Barth".)

The third section, which we have called "concrete examples", consists of individual examples to illustrate different aspects of this many-sided subject and bring out its meaning and importance. The examples show the motives and experience of joy with particular reference to the smallest units of Christian community and to Christian fringe groups and sects (Sölle and Steffensky, Cardenal and his account of Christmas in Nicaragua). There are also brief descriptions of humour and humourlessness in the Church (Schiffers, Greeley) and an account of the testimonies and background to humour and its effects in the Talmud (Tannenbaum).

The fourth section is simply a "statement" on the general theme of the issue written this time by Heinrich Böll. (On the meaning of this new section see the note immediately preceding it.)

III

We accept that our subject looks disjointed, but, in this subject above all, what possible system could guarantee the proper limits, the right connections or internal unity and completeness? In practically no other area is experience so important as in the one we have chosen, and it is experience that our contributions are trying to formulate by means of a series of test borings.

Take the question of "joy". Christianity as a religion of joy cannot be constructed artificially. Christian joy cannot be worked out from theory, nor, in the long run, can it be simulated. Christian joy is not merely natural optimism about existence. That is why joy, "earthly" pleasure in God and his promised kingdom, easily turns into an artificial or desperate pretence of naïvety, especially in Central Europe, where our whole relationship to religion is so tense. And it seems that theology has been able to talk more often and more convincingly about sadness and unhappiness, to criticize the growing superficiality of our unhappiness and the banality of our depressions with more power than it has been able to talk about the happiness of Christian joy. Is this only an illusion? Is it an accident or has it a rationale? Is it perhaps that complaints about unhappiness are easier to fit convincingly into (theological) categories? Or is the continuing power of "negative theology" only a result of theology's excessive caution, its weakness, its inability to make affirmations? After all is not joy always the offspring of mysticism, whether a mysticism of everyday life or the mysticism that bursts through the words of this "negative theology"?

Christian joy—we can say perhaps that it is the willingness to recognize this deadly world, painfully torn and hostile to itself, as capable of acceptance, as a hidden reason for thankfulness. A treatise on Christian joy would then be a treatise on the difficulty of saying yes when there is so much to which we must say no, when in fact we cannot say that all's right with the world as it is. This is why Christian joy, more than all the other Christian virtues, will have to take care that it is not misused by reactionary interests and ideologies. Its willingness to accept is in no sense an uncritical affirmation of existing earthly conditions. It includes a willingness to act firmly to make the lives of others acceptable to them and a reason for thankfulness for them. Christian joy is nothing without love. Joy without the practical interest of love is self-deception; love without the friendliness of joy degenerates into mere domination with a veneer of morality.

So how can we preserve the fragile identity of Christian joy? "Become like little children," is Jesus' advice according to New Testament sources. This only seems to lead us into further confusions since, like so many other religious symbols, that of the child seems increasingly to have lost its original force. We do have some idea of course. We know that there are tasks and questions which are "child's play" and also a childish simplicity about some very difficult questions—and about some forms of art, such as Mozart's music—and perhaps there can ultimately be no better definition of Christian joy than to say that it has the difficulty of this childish simplicity. But can we be like "little children" without becoming infantile? Can we risk such a degree of naïvety without undergoing psychic regression or simply making a pretence of the wisdom which, in Kleist's words, "ate a second time of the tree of knowledge"? Can we insist on our innocence without being cynical? Can we try to be thankful without hardening our hearts to the cry of other people's suffering? Does not the unsolved riddle of theodicy constantly overshadow every new treatise on joy?[1]

Whatever the answer, it would be impossible and wrong for us to celebrate the "feast of joy" while ignoring (excommunicating) the world's suffering. But what form does the mysticism of Christian joy take then, not just in impotent gloom and sadness, but in the passion of anger and opposition which rises in us when we, as Christians, look suffering and oppression in the face? To answer this, definitions and arguments are no longer enough; we need reports and accounts of real experience of joy. But did anyone ever read the lives of the saints as verifications of the Christian message of joy, as accounts of the "joy of a Christian man" commended to our imitation? And what about Jesus himself? What do we know about his joy? What are we

[1] For the question of theodicy in this connection see J. B. Metz, "Erlösung und Emanzipation", *Stimmen der Zeit* (March 1973); reprinted in L. Scheffczyk (ed.), *Erlösung und Emanzipation* (Freiburg, 1973).

told of it? Is it not almost his least visible attribute? To talk about this more than about any other aspect of his character are we not driven to speculation? The tradition includes reports of his grief and reports of his anger. What about his joy? What about his mirth even? Could Chesterton have been right after all in the suggestion he made at the end of his *Orthodoxy*? I apologize particularly to exegetes here for ending this article by quoting his remarks:

> The tremendous figure which fills the Gospels towers in this respect, as in every other, above all the thinkers who ever thought themselves tall. His pathos was natural, almost casual. The Stoics, ancient and modern, were proud of concealing their tears. He never concealed His tears; He showed them plainly on His open face at any daily sight, such as the far sight of His native city. Yet He concealed something. Solemn supermen and imperial diplomatists are proud of restraining their anger. He never restrained His anger. He flung furniture down the front steps of the Temple, and asked men how they expected to escape the damnation of Hell. Yet He restrained something. I say it with reverence; there was in that shattering personality a thread that must be called shyness. There was something that He hid from all men when He went up a mountain to pray. There was something that He covered constantly by abrupt silence or impetuous isolation. There was some one thing that was too great for God to show us when He walked upon our earth; and I have sometimes fancied that it was His mirth.

JOHANN BAPTIST METZ

PART I
PERSPECTIVES

David Steere

Our Capacity for Sadness and Joy: An Essay on Life before Death

SADNESS and joy are universal human emotions. They stand at the foundation of man's response to life. Joy is our basic response to love—to "en-joy" one another. Sadness is our basic response to the loss of those we love—to grieve our separation from them. Love is always bestowed against the reality of an eventual termination to the relationship it seeks. So sadness and joy necessitate one another for each to be authentic. They are emotional responses to events creating times or seasons of rejoicing and grief. We live in the presence of death and we die in the presence of life. Full moments of sadness and joy belong, thereby, to us all. We move from one to another only through full response to each in its time.

This *Concilium* explores a diminishing ability of contemporary man to be both sad and joyful. We begin with the assumption that both emotions deserve full expression. As the Johannine author puts it, "You have sorrow now, but your hearts will rejoice." (John 16. 22.) We also assume the discomforting fact that the converse is likewise true. Our focus is on the climates we share which permit or inhibit our ability to participate in joy and sadness to a point which satisfies our basic human needs for their expression.

I. PERMISSION: SOCIAL AND PERSONAL

Permission is the medium through which sadness and joy may receive full expression. Each culture trains its people to live together through an elaborate system of permissions and injunctions. Permissions grant people freedom to do as they wish. The model is a parent telling a small child, "It's all right to do that." Behind every permission stands a system of values which separates "all right" behaviours from "not all right" ones, usually with a hierarchy that stretches from "best" to "worst".

Injunctions command and forbid certain behaviours directly. They prescribe our responses explicitly. The model is the parent telling the small child, "Always say 'thank you'" or "Don't ever push anyone on the stairs." A workable social order without both injunctions and permissions is inconceivable. The most powerful ones are delivered through non-verbal acts and rarely, if ever, put into words. Injunctions against incest are delivered by glances, scowls, quick movements away, and sounds of disgust rather than actually telling the little girl she shouldn't engage in sexual acts with her father or her brother.

Sadness and joy are emotions. They come as waves of feeling within us. We express them through emoting, erupting, emptying. They come as a response to concrete events and cannot be commanded by injunctions. A mother drags her small boy down the lighted midway of a carnival. He cries at the top of his lungs. "You wanted to come," she exclaims. "Now you are going to enjoy yourself if it kills you!" Her injunction only heightens his unhappiness.

Joy and sadness come only through permission. Permissions give licence to author whatever activities we choose within prescribed limits. For example, "You can play anywhere in the neighbourhood until dark." Permissions grant the freedom to make our own responses in accord with what is within us.

Two types of permissions are necessary to express joy and sadness: *social permission* and *personal permission*. The two constantly intertwine to govern how much emotion we can experience and express. John is filled with joy at the birth of his first son. A measure of enjoyment is his as he savours the news alone. But his feelings beg for expression to others about him—his wife, his family, his friends, perhaps even an unknown companion on the street. Eventually he may shape the meaning of his joy through Baptism or Christening in a church or some formal social gathering to sanction the event. John's experience of joy is governed first by how much social permission he meets to encourage its expression in the community of persons around him. Social permission to feel is granted in community through the varying degrees of licence awarded for free participation in that feeling with others.

No amount of social permission alone, however, can elicit joy from John. His own personal permission to feel is constituted by the particular structure of injunctions and permissions he has acquired over a lifetime. He may have permission to laugh loudly, to show his warmth, to tell others he loves them. Or significant figures from his past may have delivered injunctions against making too much noise, exhibiting closeness, or having too much fun. Magical qualities are often associated with injunctions which prohibit feeling. "Pride comes before a fall" forms a powerful invective against too free an enjoyment of "proud papa" feelings. For if pride bespeaks the presence of impending disaster, better to curtail the positive feelings as if to magically fend off an anticipated fall than to run the risk of too much satisfaction. Social permission governs the extent we are met by others who will grant us expression of joy and sadness. Personal permission governs our own capacity to participate in these feelings, whether we enter them fully or withdraw from them in some form of preoccupation.

Religion has historically provided the ground for evaluating all life experience, bestowing meaning to major events within its course, and offering opportunities for corporate expression of our responses at each stage. The Church becomes a grantor of social permissions to its believers and the protector of corporate injunctions deemed necessary to preserve life. The Church has always sought to structure occasions to celebrate events deemed joyful. The birth of a child is celebrated in baptism, coming into adulthood is celebrated in confirmation, marriage with sacrament or service, and high days or seasons with feasting and worship. Permission to be sorrowful has also been a continuing occasion within all believing bodies. The sorrow of sin is expressed through forms of confession, the sorrow of grief through the funeral, and the sorrow of our own death through last rites and pastoral care. A diminishing capacity for people to be joyful and sad evidences a reduction of sacred permissions we have always sought to bestow.

II. THE SACRED AND THE PROFANE

Much has been written about the emergence of secularism in our age. Secular man who organizes his life apart from God and creates his own meaning is opposed to religious man who opens himself to God as author and revealer of life. The debate surrounding sacred and secular world views tends to obscure an inherently religious dimension in all our efforts to value and order life together. Mircea Eliade describes a common thread in all premodern religions, originating in man's efforts to situate himself meaningfully in time and space.[1] Initially, premodern man encountered the world as an amorphous mass of time and space. This infinite number of neutral places and countless series of undifferentiated moments in succession Eliade calls the *profane world*. Archaic man believed that the *sacred* manifested itself in the primitive void as a reality wholly different, creating form, order and meaning. The sacred gave man the power to participate in the world with purpose.

Man becomes religious at the point where he drives a stake and proceeds to create a world of meaning around it. Archaic man often lifted a world pole (*axis mundi*) as a sacred centre. It may have been stationary or portable. It may have been literally a pole or a mountain or a temple. Whatever, it marked the centre of his world. Around it a known world (*cosmos*) was created out of chaos. The sacred centre delineated safe and in-habited territories from uninhabited ones. Around it space was ordered with appointed purpose—fields for crops, woods for hunting, water for fishing, villages for homes.

Time was likewise given meaning and order around the centre. There archaic man believed he broke through the meaningless succession of moments and stood in communication with the gods. Certain times were more important than others calling for specific acts to honour them. All time was to be spent in accord

[1] Mircea Eliade, *The Sacred and the Profane* (New York, 1959); *Cosmos and History* (New York, 1959), *Myth and Reality* (New York, 1963); *Myths, Dreams, and Mysteries* (New York, 1960).

with values realized and celebrated around the *axis mundi*. Through worship the sacred structured time providing paradigms or models for living. Myths about the meaning and purpose of creation were told and retold. Legends about forefathers were repeated to elevate the range of human activities and feelings valued in the community. Stories were told about all of life, about birth, about ancestors defending their territory, about how the law was given, and about what people lived for and died for.

Life took shape as an effort to imitate these models. The result was a constantly growing centre of social permissions and injunctions serving as the pattern for all significant activities. If God worked for the benefit of others, archaic man was enjoined to work for the benefit of others. If the law of the fathers forbade killing, he was forbidden to kill. If God were just, he must be just. If God laughed, he could laugh, and if God cried, he could cry.

Every religious institution conveys an evolving set of permissions and injunctions. Injunctions tend to take shape as law designed to protect the community. Permissions contain the more vital designation of possibilities and freedom as we occupy time and space. For instance, how far are we permitted to travel within the world? In premodern days, the cosmos may have ended at a dense forest or a river that delineated the extent of permissible distance to move from the centre. In Columbus' day, the cosmos ended at an unknown shelf somewhere in the Atlantic beyond which lay chaos. In our day it extends to the moon, at least. Permissions provide protection within their limitations, delineating the perimeters within which it is "all right" to move.

Similar dimensions of safe entrance and extent of movement regulate all our efforts to occupy time and space. How far can we extend our personal contacts? Does our cosmos include persons of a different colour, language or faith? How much of our time do we spend working, playing, learning, dancing, meditating, etc.? How far are we permitted to go in each? How free am I to be sad? How far can I safely move into grief without fear of becoming lost from the cosmos? How much pleasure may I experience safely without becoming engulfed by joy?

Stories of the faith—historical, legendary, or mythical—become the major conveyors of these dimensions of permission. As we hear what others have done, the range of possibilities governing safe entrance and freedom to explore are opened for structuring our own lifetime and energy.

III. CONCORDANCE AND DISCORDANCE

The sacred manifests itself in the world through concordance or harmony. What we do in time and space is in accord with what we celebrate at the centre and vice versa. The profane emerges wherever there is discordance between our cosmos and human activities. Discordance renders us aliens without freedom to enjoy or explore. Our capacity to respond with joy or sadness is altered. Our responses as Christians—Catholic, Protestant, or Orthodox—must be considered within the context of three other basic human emotions.

Anger is one response. Blind, materialistic squandering of lifetime and life-space is discordant with all we hold sacred. Alliances of power which exploit the poor, pollute the earth, and protect the privileged anger us. Each emotion carries with it a particular movement or motion of expression. The movement of anger is to attack. We become agents of change, attacking power with reason, with justice, and with counter-power seeking victory for a cause through communal organization "against" injustice which will not yield. During seasons of attack, our capacity for joy and sorrow becomes secondary and diminished. Celebration is of victory, won competitively over part of the world which is estranged to us. Sorrow in our opponent's failures is hollow and mingled with the satisfaction of enhancing our own position.

Fear is a second basic response. War splits our cosmos asunder. Naked power, omnipotently possessed to repress and exterminate, produces the terror of Jewish peoples in Hitler's Europe. The movement of fear is to withdraw. Escape reigns in this time. Joy is beyond reach and there is insufficient time to really be sorrowful. All life energy is directed to survival.

The third basic emotion is boredom. It is the most insidious response to the profane for it is the product of a slow, pro-

1. attack   (anger)
2. w/draw   (fear)
3. drift   (boredm)

gressive evolution of meaninglessness which quietly renders us impotent to act purposefully in time and space. Our industrialization and technology grind ever forward, separating us from the natural rhythms of a life past, making all time and space the same. Urbanization rips us from our roots of primary, personal relationships and reduces us to the anonymous, isolated patterns of city life. Corporate life segments our relationships so we cease to know one another except in fleeting roles and restricted pieces of a lifetime. Economic necessities to produce and consume create a frantic and fabricated need to "enjoy" materials with increasing cost and decreasing satisfaction. The movement of boredom is drifting. An aimless existence of undifferentiated experiences in succession renders us captive to the mundane repetition of routine. Our capacity to be genuinely sad or joyful is silently anesthetized into indifference.

Our search is for a Christian model to live in the world with increased capacity for joy and sadness. One option is to withdraw in fear to our own sacred centre, perhaps making occasional forays out to attack its dissonance. This is a profane surrender of our cosmos. The other is to leave our sacred centre in search of all we may join and include within our cosmos. It is to claim concordance wherever it may be found. What appears to be secular may or may not be. Whatever we are not driven to attack or withdraw from in fear has potential for *en-joy-ment.*

We have a story of Jesus from our own sacred centre as a paradigm or model for this activity. It occurs at the end of Luke's account of the transfiguration experience. (Lk. 9. 49–50.) Jesus has come into touch with God and the figures of Moses and Elijah whom he follows. Peter, James and John want to build three booths there on the mountain and remain at their *axis mundi.* But the task is clearly to return to the valley of the world below, to cast out demons from a child, to move on to Jerusalem, and to put behind them arguments about who is greatest in the new kingdom (cosmos). Then John shows up announcing he has discovered a man casting out demons in Jesus' name who is not a follower and has forbidden him to continue. Jesus' poignant plea is to include rather than exclude this unknown figure, "for he that is not against you is for you."

IV. RESPONSIBILITY AND PREOCCUPATION

Social permissions to respond with all our fundamental human emotions except boredom are found in the paradigms of Jesus' life. Anger is expressed by Jesus' movement to drive the money changers from the temple. Sorrow is expressed in his tears for Lazarus. Fear, but not withdrawal, is expressed in Gethsemane. And joy in feasting and fellowship appears even in the face of the end. Our model of Jesus' life contains an amazing freedom of responses to each time or season or event. Each response is full with meaning and emotion. There is no room for boredom in the new kingdom.

This is a model for responsibility—viewing ourselves as responsive beings capable of responding to all of life, including death. H. Richard Niebuhr captures its essence in his concept of the *responsible self*.[2] The responsible self always responds to a context of the action of life upon him in accordance (concordance) with his interpretation of that act, with clear anticipation of what response will come to his response, and within a continuing effort to establish and maintain community (cosmos).

Preoccupation occupies the present with something else which diminishes our capacity to respond fully. Whenever we permit our response to be governed by the dimensions of past or future times, we surrender our ability to make a free response to the moment. The potential for novelty and creativity gives way to routine or expectation. We are subtly robbed of our potential for change.

Preoccupations manifest themselves as time-binders which cast clauses of "until" or "after" over the present, carrying us out of the moment to something remembered or anticipated. None of us lives without them. In milder forms they may be highly pleasurable and valuable to motivation. "After I was married, I really began to live." "Until I complete my training, I can't do the work I want." As full-blown preoccupations, however, such clauses function to truncate or even dismantle our responsiveness to life. For example, "Until we have overcome starvation, no person may be joyful," appears at first glance to be highly

[2] H. Richard Niebuhr, *The Responsible Self* (New York, Evanston, and London, 1963), pp. 47–67.

moral. Not so noble is "After what they did, I'll never trust anyone again." But each injunction extends a preoccupation with one time or season of human experience into every time or season of human experience. Each casts a powerful binding effect upon our permission to make full and new responses in the present. The responsible self is not bound by "until" or "after" clauses from any time or season of life.

A recovered capacity for sadness and joy in our time is contingent upon creating climates of permission to make full entrance into these emotions at their appropriate time. The pastoral task is to disengage "until" and "after" clauses which form prohibitive injunctions. We address a complex system extending throughout both religious and secular life. "I can't relax until I've got it made." "After my husband's death, I haven't wanted to live." "After you've tried forty times, you give up." "Until I know what he's going to do, I can't do anything." "After you've been through as much as I have, you resign yourself to the inevitable." "Until we make this world a better place, nobody's going to be happy." "After you've worked a lifetime, you get to take things easy."

V. AMELIA

Preoccupations are governed by debilitating injunctions which close off our responsiveness with "until" and "after" clauses. Here intertwining levels of social permission and personal permission need to be extended, granting the person a new freedom to respond in the present. A case study of Amelia, a twenty-nine-year-old married woman without children who comes for pastoral counselling points out the issues.[3] Amelia is mildly depressed most of the time. When so, she eats compulsively to the point of being ninety pounds overweight. She is unhappy in her job as a social worker where she feels inadequate as a counsellor to under-privileged families. She is unhappy in her marriage where she quarrels with her husband who has been fired from

[3] Amelia's case is drawn with permission from the author's own pastoral counselling records with sufficient changes in name and facts to prevent her identification.

a number of jobs. She seldom enjoys herself or feels worthwhile. She has left the Church because she has lost her faith.

Amelia joins a counselling group where people work toward changing things they do not like in their lives. At first she concentrates on losing weight, gaining confidence, and establishing a relationship with her husband who gets and holds a permanent job. Everyone comes to know her as a person who tries hard yet remains chronically depressed. Then a series of events reveal the "until" and "after" dimensions governing her present life.

Amelia's mother becomes ill and near the point of death. She has Huntington's Chorea, one of the few diseases which appear to be transmitted directly through hereditary factors as a Mendelian characteristic. About fifty per cent of the offspring in each generation contract it. It is an untreatable, debilitating disease that appears between ages thirty-five and forty, marked by progressive physical and mental deterioration, impaired memory and judgment, eventual loss of speech and bodily control, and death. Once the chain of heredity is broken, the offspring are not likely to develop Huntington's Chorea. Amelia hoped her mother would escape. When she learned her mother contracted it nine years ago, she went to a state mental hospital with a depression of psychotic proportion. Now she lives with a fifty/fifty chance of getting the disease herself within six years.

After Amelia learned of her mother's illness, she formed a profound preoccupation. She could only wait "until" she learned whether she would get it. Her life was marked by a quiet, fearful withdrawal. Until she learned, she could not have children. Until she learned, she could not entrust herself to closeness with her husband, only to face giving him up. Until she learned, further education was a meaningless waste. A cloud of transiency was cast over all her moments, which prohibited full responses to anything.

First Amelia's mother is placed in a nursing home. Amelia's father drinks heavily and is unable to help in the care. Then Amelia's mother dies. The persons in the group around her sense her distress, but she remains withdrawn and non-communicative, as if stoically resigned to fate. Her husband tries to talk to her but does not succeed. It is as if everyone has been dragged into an unwitting conspiracy to avoid and deny any feelings seeking expression.

VI. SOCIAL PERMISSION

Finally, one member of the group becomes weary of the conspiracy. Awkwardly he blurts out his feelings that Amelia has an unfair advantage over everyone. Her situation is so grim no one can expect her to respond. Why should she be given licence to withdraw and give up? Other members of the group express shock at so straightforward a violation of their unvoiced pact of avoidance. How can one be so cruel? "Hell," comes the response, "our parents all die and we're all gonna die too. Why should she have a corner on futility?"

Unlike her defenders, Amelia is not offended. She expresses relief and begins to talk. Suddenly she has been met by someone giving her permission to express herself. Nowhere else has this happened. At the clinic, she is a professional counsellor, and professionals who help others are assumed to be strong enough to handle their own problems. Amelia's friends "understand" this is a difficult time. They ignore her silence and remark "how well she is holding up" after her mother's death.

When Amelia went to church, she heard a number of messages. One was to "have faith," which she had interpreted since childhood as praying and believing that prayers would be answered. Her prayers for her mother were unanswered, and she has no faith that her "faith" can deliver her from a similar death. Another message was "to believe in eternal life beyond death." "I want to live now," she says, "but I can't, knowing this awful thing is always there." Stories of Jesus' suffering strike no chords of meaning for her. "I don't even have the dignity of suffering for others," she remarks. "They don't tell stories about that. They talk a lot about love and justice, but no one wants to talk about those things with me."

Amelia has ended her withdrawal and begun to talk. The others grant permission. But how much bitterness, anger, and fear is it safe to permit? As much as the psalmists expressed against their enemies or against God? There is contempt for her father who abused the family while drinking and never cared for her mother or her. There is irritation toward other people who are different and do not understand. There is anger for her husband who still wants to enjoy himself in spite of her despair. The answer to how much is in terms of the amount of expression required by Amelia herself to complete this time or season and move to the next.

Beneath the anger, a softening appears. Amelia finally gives vent to a profound sadness which she fears will engulf her. She permits herself to weep over her mother's death and over the prospect of losing her own life. She moves fully into her grief for the first time, and she is afraid because she has spent so much time defending against the impact of such emotion.

Here we are not without some knowledge of the human need to make full entrance into sadness. Erich Lindemann observed the necessity of people to do *grief work* when they lose a loved one, to cry, to be preoccupied with the image of the lost person, to express irrational anger about their loss, to declare guilt over times when they failed in the relationship, etc.[4] If permitted, we work our way through grief as with labour in the birth of a child, freeing ourselves to move on. If forbidden, we become preoccupied, experiencing delayed grief reactions or depressions extending far into later seasons of life.

Permission to be sad is given by others around us who meet us in our grief and accompany us through it. In the Gethsemane story, Jesus reads the handwriting on the wall. He grieves his own death and separation. And he hungers for James and Peter and John to remain awake and "watch with him." All our impulses to prematurely enhearten or cut short the other's grief as if to take the struggle from them work against this essential need. Suppose one of us could take the place of Peter or James or John? What would we say to Jesus in Gethsemane? "There, there, Lord, you remember how you taught us to have faith." Or "It's going to be all right, Lord, God will raise you up." Or "Keep a stiff upper lip, Jesus, we have to see these things through, you know." We extend hope by creating a climate of

[4] Erich Lindemann, M.D., "Symptomatology and the Management of Acute Grief," *The Journal of Pastoral Care,* V (1951), pp. 19–31. Reprinted from *The American Journal of Psychiatry,* CI (September 1944).

permission to make full entrance into sadness and to express it to the point of satiation.

VII. Personal Permission

Amelia has already broken some of the personal injunctions with which she has lived for years. For example, when grandmother died of Huntington's Chorea, mother said, "Don't cry." The family was not permitted to cry because of the awesome fear involved in facing the legacy which the disease extended over mother's life. Recovering a full capacity for sadness and joy involves, for Amelia, breaking a series of such injunctions that inhibit her responsiveness.

Psychiatrist Eric Berne has described this structure of personal injunctions as taking the shape of a *life script*.[5] In our formative years each of us has been handed a script to read or a life plan by which we structure our responses in time and space. Our script is like a part to play in life, specifying the kind of character we are to develop in dramatic exchange with others from first curtain to final curtain.

Life scripting governs the range of personal responses we have in the same way that corporate acts, stories, and rites govern the social permissions we extend to one another. Pastoral care addresses the climate we create in our corporate life. Pastoral counselling addresses the personal permissions we need to become free to respond. Amelia's life scripting is filled with injunctions that sanction her withdrawal from others. While she was very small, mother cared for her own invalid mother there in the house. This made Amelia different. She could not bring her friends in to play. Loud noises or laughter disturbed Grandma, who was "always sick." Mother was frequently tired, irritable, and sullen. Father felt shut out, often drinking himself into a stupor. Powerful injunctions were delivered to Amelia in this setting which, when put into words, read something like this: "You are different than other people." "You can never be

[5] Eric Berne, M.D., *What Do You Say After You Say Hello?: The Psychology of Human Destiny* (New York, 1972).

happy when someone is sick." "You can never be happy until you know you don't have Huntington's disease." "Once you get Huntington's disease, you are better off dead." "When there is sickness around, never get close to (intimate with) anyone."

Amelia's freedom to respond to her present life differently is contingent upon breaking these injunctions. This is the province of pastoral counselling—granting personal permissions to respond differently. The task is entirely different from issuing a new set of commands or prohibitions. For Amelia cannot be commanded to en-joy her life, to permit closeness with her husband, to care for herself, or to devote herself to education or work. But we can expose and identify the injunctions above, which prohibit these responses, freeing Amelia to do as she wishes.

Amelia's group slowly manages to extend these permissions which can probably be extended in as many different ways as there are people. The member who challenges her "differentness" opens the door. So she is the only person in the room with a fifty/fifty chance of a debilitating disease in six years. After we have joined her sadness fully, what then? The "differentness" between her and the others is reduced to a matter of duration in a transient life filled with all the uncertainties everybody faces. Amelia's withdrawal is weakened. May the others laugh in her presence and enjoy her smile? The answer is "yes." And already bonds of affection have silently been formed in spite of her injunctions against closeness.

Amelia's radical change comes weeks later on a day she subtly decides to break all the injunctions from her past. It happens in a relatively simple question that emerges from another group member. What would she do if she learned that she would never get Huntington's disease? Amelia found herself free to respond clearly in the moment. She would go back to school and increase her professional skills, completing a graduate degree. She would plan to purchase a home and consider adopting children. And she would become attractive by completing her weight loss, permitting herself to work out her marriage with her husband. And what, asked the group, would she do if she knew today she would have the disease ten years from now?

"The very same thing," she responded, with an authentic and en-joyable smile.

VIII. LIFE BEFORE DEATH

We all live in the presence of death and we all die in the presence of life. The valiant taste of death more than once, and in tasting, they move on to affirm life before death. A number of other affirmations follow naturally.

An emphasis on life after death dulls our capacity to experience both joy and sadness. The sadness of death is treated as a prelude to eternal life. The joy of life is reduced to a transient facsimile of another life beyond.

If we disregard death, we disregard a vital part of life. If we disregard life, we make death an unrealistic blessing which it is not. The former is blatantly naïve. The latter is suicidal in spirit. Both do violence to reality. A full drink at the well of sadness or joy satiates our thirst to deal with these realities sufficiently to renew our journey to the next place.

Life is a gift and the essence of grace. Is death also a similar gift? We do not know. Truly no man knows. To embrace life is to hate death which pulls apart the embrace. A life which awaits death is fearfully restricted by a vain effort to fend off pain at its end. A life which hastens the end is a tragic and fearful squandering of precious lifetime.

Joy comes in the resurrection of the body, in lifting up life in the body. The resurrection story gives us permission to enjoy, not despise, the life of the body. Not only is God incarnate, but the body defies death. Preoccupation with youthfulness despises age. Preoccupation with the fear of bodily pleasure denies joy. Preoccupation with self-control denies the God-given gift of grace-ful emotions. To respond fully within our lifetime is to embrace our transience with moments of Epicurean realism and say, "I am free to enjoy all that has become enjoyable within my cosmos."

O grave, where is thy victory?
O death, where is thy sting?

1 Cor. 15. 55

For I am persuaded that neither death, nor life, nor angels, nor
principalities, nor things present, nor things to come, nor powers,
nor height, nor depth, nor anything else in all creation, will be
able to separate us from the love of God in Christ Jesus our Lord.

Romans 8. 38, 39

This is the day which the Lord has made;
Let us rejoice and be glad in it.

Ps. 118. 24

Michael Landmann

Melancholies of Fulfilment

I. THE SADNESS OF BEAUTY

FROM the time of Winckelmann, German classicism has been aware of, and worried about, the fact that in the faces of Greek statues, alongside harmony and remoteness, a certain sadness can be seen.[1] Winckelmann himself noticed the thoughtful seriousness which cast a shadow on their serenity, but, like Herder, he saw it as no more than a source of aesthetic intensity. On the other hand, Fritz Stolberg explained the melancholy of Greek man as resulting from the fact that, as a pagan, he was at the mercy of impermanence, with no promise or hope of an otherworldly redemption. "Even over the faces of the eternal divine youths, there hovers as it were a dark cloud, the thought of death." Goethe mocked this view of Stolberg's in an epigram, but Adam Müller supported him.

The connection of Greek melancholy with the idea of death appears in another variant in the age of Goethe. The reason for the shadow on the serene and peaceful brows of the gods is, we are told, that, though themselves immortal, they are grieving for the death of their darlings, men, which they cannot avert. "Beauty too must die ..." (Schiller). Others see the position reversed: just as men envy the gods the smooth flow of their existence, so the gods envy men's mixture of good and bad fortune. The static perfection of Greek man, as well as the Greek gods, in his imperturbable *ataraxia* and windless *galēnē*, is

[1] This section is based on Walter Rehm, *Götterstille und Göttertrauer* (Munich, 1951).

31

exclusion from life. His detached self-sufficiency, unlike that of Empedocles' sphere, which delighted in its isolation, can take the form of loneliness a torment of longing for fellow feeling.

Herder was the first to introduce an historical note into these reflections, believing that *we* introduced the note of sadness into the classical statues because we knew how transitory this flowering was. (This idea that we project our own melancholy deserves attention in its own right.) In contrast, Novalis said that the Greek gods were sad because they themselves were haunted by a dim awareness of the inevitability of their death. This idea was taken up by Schelling and later by Lasaulx. In 1809, Schelling spoke of a veil of melancholy covering the whole of nature, not to be lifted until Christ. In his *Philosophie der Offenbarung,* he goes on to talk about the esoteric belief among the Greeks in a future reign of Dionysus, and about "the awareness which even in the most abandoned pleasure never left them, that all this glory would one day fade, this whole beautiful world of appearance would one day pass away and yield to a higher, truthful clarity. This idea is the cause of the melancholy which runs like a sweet poison through the finest works of the Hellenes, especially their sculpture." Even apart from this sort of theology of history, Schelling believed that perfection of form destroyed itself at its peak because it became merged at that point with the infinite. According to Schleiermacher, perfection brings every nature close to its opposite. The idea of the close proximity of beauty and death, that the peak of beauty is the beginning of decay and the longing for beauty a longing for death, runs through the romantic movement. Perfection was not possible without pain.

Hegel's phrase "the painfulness of the divine peace" sums up his view that the Greek god, through his aims and actions, shares in the human, the accidental, the limitations of the finite, and this brings him into contradiction with his own power and dignity. The lonely bliss of the statues' stillness and the quiet marks of sadness are a vain attempt to reconcile this contradiction. In Kierkegaard's romantic-idealist speculations the Spirit, as first revealed by Christianity, was not part of the Greek synthesis. "This is the source of an assurance, a calm solemnity, in Greek beauty, and at the same time of a fear, probably unnoticed by the Greeks, although their plastic beauty quickened in it. Because the Spirit is excluded, Greek beauty is without pain, but for the same reason it contains a pain which is inexplicably deep."

From such flights the anti-classical and realistic movement more truly representative of the nineteenth century steps back. It no longer isolates art from its basis in life, but uses this as the way to a new understanding. For Jacob Burckhardt, the dazzling works of art were ideals standing out against a frightful political reality of evil. The sadness of the gods was the intrusion of this unredeemed and guilt-laden Greek reality into the world of art.

Before these profound and extravagant interpretations from the heroic age of the German mind, the late-comer with thoughts of his own to add hesitates.

The Greeks discovered the "autonomy" of the individual who is guided by his own reason. Unlike later philosophical exaltations of autonomy, however, they were also aware, from the very beginning, of the limits of the powers of reason. Gods and fate work against our plans. Even if we achieve our goals we achieve them not just by our own efforts, but also because these incalculable powers allow us to. Even happiness is something that "happens" to us.[2] In this interpretation the sadness of the Greek statues would be a reflection of this knowledge. The first discovery of autonomy and human nature is accompanied by the painful realization that its range is limited, that it comes up against things beyond its reach and in opposition to it. Greek man was sad at the weakness of the principle in which he placed his trust, sad at the "limits of human nature".

By discovering autonomy, the Greeks also discovered the individual. Georg Simmel, however, in his philosophy of death, has taught us that the capacity for death increases in the same proportion as individual differentiation, and is indeed its indicator. The more sharply defined the characteristics of a creature have been, the less of it remains at its destruction, the

[2] Cf. M. Landmann, "Virtus und Fatum", in *Pluralität und Antinomie* (Munich, 1963) and "Eine Lanze für das Schicksal", in *Das Ende des Individuums* (Stuttgart, 1971).

more irretrievably is it lost to the world. No other thing can replace it. What is more individual is also more mortal. "Being able to die is the sign of a higher existence." This is why tragedy shows us the hero as a man falling part, to reveal his greatness. Tragedy has no better way of confirming his eminence, no more profound way of celebrating him, than by being tragic and making him fall. What tragedy presents as a sequence, sculpture squeezes into a moment. The threat to the individual, precisely because he is an individual, from death, the fall to which he is exposed through his very uniqueness and value, is foreshadowed in the statue as sadness.[3]

II. The Sadness of Victory

Like a frost on the bloom of perfect form, a chill strikes the triumph of victory. This applies in both the literal and figurative sense.

In the baroque period, the paradigm of the melancholic man was seen in Nero, the ruler of the greatest empire in history.[4] For Pascal, himself one of the fathers of "philosophical melancholy", Nero became a symbol of loneliness and boredom, of the man full of compassion surrounded by the splendour of a throne. Again in Kierkegaard we find the emperor led by power into aesthetic complacency; he can no longer undividedly seek the good and as a result is full of secret fear and listlessness. There is a similar picture in the French literature of the period —because his resources are limitless, because no one opposes him, he falls into cruelty and licentiousness, under which he then suffers.

Nero's counterpart in a quite different sphere is the artist. Aristotle and Cicero in their day knew the melancholy of the spirit, and the Renaissance took it up. In the Middle Ages, *acedia* was the deadly sin, arising out of estrangement from God. It was the monk's disease. But in Petrarch and the Florentine humanists it underwent ennoblement as a this-worldly psy-

[3] Cf. M. Landmann, "Zeit und Tod", in *Ursprungsbild und Schöpfertat* (Munich, 1966).
[4] This section is based on Walter Rehm, "Jacobsen und die Schwermut", in *Experimentum medietatis* (Munich, 1947). See also Wolf Lepennies, *Melancholie und Gesellschaft* (Frankfurt, 1972), pp. 46 ff. and 215 ff.

chological condition which distinguished creative people from ordinary mortals. Melancholy became the tribute that genius had to pay for its profundity and intellectuality. The man of genius was allowed to enjoy melancholy, which reinforced his self-esteem.

Victory is a relation, and must be analysed as one member of a whole in which its counterpart is the defeated. What is basic is not sadness, but the victor's jubilation, pride and mercilessness. There is also an art which derives from this attitude and which today is accordingly suspect. It was Herbert Read who pointed out that wherever Doric columns had stood the cries of the slaves had rung out unheard. Religious or ethical feeling checked unrestrained celebration of victory at a quite early date. When Eurycleia was about to rejoice over the dead suitors, Odysseus stopped her: "Rejoice in your heart, old woman, and hold back your shouts of joy; it is wrong to triumph over the bodies of the dead."[5]

This may have arisen out of fear of the spirits of the victims, but also acquired ethical backing. According to a midrash, when the Egyptians were drowned in the sea, the angels wanted to sing a psalm to God, but God said, "Men whom I created perish in the sea, and you want to celebrate?"[6] These are the first stirrings which were later to be drawn on by those who set themselves up as defenders of the conquered against the victors.

Against the victors. In social and political terms that means for the slaves against the masters, for the oppressed against the ruling class, for those who produce surplus value against the exploiters who deprive them of it. But it also means against a history which is written by the survivors and forgets those who were sacrificed, whom it throws on to what Lenin called the "scrap-heap of history", a history which presents success as if it had also had spiritual and moral arguments on its side even though in fact what was unable to prevail in the course of history may have been better (Ernst Bloch's "future in the past"). For history, too, the general "discovery of the underprivileged" brings with it a "new sensibility". Walter Benjamin prefaces his

[5] Homer, *Odyssey* XXII, pp. 411–12.
[6] From Micha Josef Bin Gurion, *Die Sagen der Juden* (Frankfurt, 1962), p. 464.

seventh thesis on the philosophy of history with a quotation from Brecht,[7] but he might have done better to choose another statement, namely "What kind of a world is it where it's almost a crime to talk about flowers because it means not talking about so many horrors?"[8] Benjamin goes on to talk about historicist historians' natural sympathy with the victor. Since today's rulers are the heirs of those who conquered before them this identification with the victors always benefits them. Therefore, says Benjamin, Marxist history writing, based on a desire to overthrow the rulers, must be different.

Benjamin extends this idea from political to cultural history. "According to traditional practice, the spoils are carried along in the procession. They are called cultural treasures, and an historical materialist views them with cautious detachment. For without exception the cultural treasures he surveys have an origin which he cannot contemplate without horror. They owe their existence not only to the efforts of the great minds and talents who have created them, but also to the anonymous toil of their contemporaries. There is no document of civilization which is not at the same time a document of barbarism.... The historical materialist therefore ... regards it as his task to brush history against the grain."

Benjamin's argument seems to become strangely confused, however, when he explains the process of empathy which takes place in the historicist as the result of *acedia,* sadness. It is hard to see what reason for sadness an historian would have if he completely lacks awareness of "those who are lying prostrate", of the barbarism of the world. This sadness seems more obviously appropriate to the "horror" of the historical materialist, who refuses to give way to the fascination of the " triumphal procession" of rulers. It looks as though Benjamin has got his notes out of order in the haste of producing the final version.

The new sort of history writing proposed by Benjamin will, unlike existing histories, take up the cause of the defeated, but it will do this not just for the sake of justice and not only be-

[7] Walter Benjamin, *Illuminations* (London, 1973), pp. 258–9.
[8] I am indebted for references to Benjamin in particular, but also for other remarks on this essay, to Ernst Erdös (Zürich).

cause the conquerors of the past are just as much the enemies of the Marxist as the rulers of the present, and he takes the side of the lost cause. Another reason is that the lost cause points forward to us and our revolutionary activity. It is the seed embedded in the misrepresentation of the defeated which waited for us to make it grow. In saving the cause by bringing it to life as historians, we are not taking the side of the underdog, but pointing to true greatness and the true future. For Benjamin, however, this was part of a larger context, which he shared for years with Ernst Bloch and drew him to others besides the defeated. In his literary work also, in a similar way to the French symbolists' "spleen", he tried to unearth what prevailing interests passed over, what traditional styles left out, what cut across contemporary patterns. The effect of these patterns was to "blind", and therefore what broke into them was also a break-through, the objective proletariat of things, which can upset the foundations of a world, the herald of a world as yet only dimly glimpsed.

There is another sense in which the historical process has conquerors and conquered. This comes about if it is regarded as an accelerating progress, or even if one believes only that the present state will be replaced by a future higher one. This puts those who lived in the past at a disadvantage and may even do them an injustice. An optimistic belief in progress which goes beyond the individual finds consolation for the torment of the fathers in the happiness of the sons, but what use is this consolation to those who have fallen silent and been forgotten?[9] Are we really condemned to provide the elements out of which a later totality will, as Schiller suggested, be composed? The cry of the martyrs is no less loud for being enshrined in the hearts of the working class. This is an open wound in all future-centred religions and all teleological visions of a perfected world.

This is connected with one of the reasons for the Pharisees' introduction of the originally unbiblical belief in the resurrection. Why, they argued, should only those who have the good fortune to live at the time of the Messiah see the messianic kingdom, while whole races of the past, the most eminent men

[9] Cf. J. B. Metz, "Erlösung und Emanzipation", *Stimmen der Zeit,* 191, No. 3 (1973).

of prehistory, had no share in it?[10] Their resurrection is an ethical postulate; it is their due in justice. This argument occurs again in Ernst Bloch's *Geist der Utopie*. The risen body cannot of course undo the pains of those who do not rise, but it offers compensation for them. To put it in other terms, the messianic meal is a sad as well as a joyful occasion, because it comes so late and because the dead are excluded from it. An eschatology which forgot its covenant solidarity with the dead, failed to remember their sufferings which could never be wiped out, would be immoral. The cross still stands in the new heaven and the new earth. As Ivan Karamazov says in his tirade against the harmony of the world, "I was a believer, and I want to see for myself. And if I'm dead by that time, let them resurrect me, for if it all happens without me it will be too unfair. Surely the reason for my suffering was not that I as well as my evil deeds and sufferings may serve as manure for some future harmony for someone else. I want to see with my own eyes the lion lie down with the lamb and the murdered man rise up and embrace his murderer." The attitude appears in a totally secular form in Zamyatin's novel *We* after the Russian revolution of 1905: "Why should I be hanged so that the workers of the thirty-second century will no longer go without food and pleasures?" He wants to be more than a rung on the ladder, refuses to accept that a generation should be used as fuel for the future. He gives up and becomes an Epicurean.

III. THE SADNESS OF SUCCESS

Victory resulted in a sadness arising out of the relation to the defeated. With success it arises again out of another relation, out of the relation to the phase before success, to the longing and the preparation. The goal once reached enters into a hostile tension with its image during the approach to it.

In this sense "the melancholy of fulfilment" is the secret key to our age. We live in an "era of fulfilments". If we take examples from socialism, it triumphed in Russia in 1917 and after the Second World War in Eastern Europe and China. But

[10] Cf. M. Landmann, "Unsterblichkeit und Geschichtlichkeit", in *Urspringsbild und Schöpfertat*.

whereas in a previous period Franz Mehring could still say, "We are sure of our victory and look forward to our future," from Alexandra Kollontal[11] to Rossanna Rossanda[12] the cry goes up that the victory was a cheat and a ground for despair rather than satisfaction. The reality brings either the ideal or any realization into question, or puts the ideal a level higher. "Was this what we hoped for?" is the question now, "Was this what we fought for?" "Was it worth it?" Arthur Koestler's "God that failed" was certainly able to eliminate a number of historically determined weaknesses, but he alone cannot change the general historical outlook. "Alienation" remains the fate of the modern age even under socialism. And then, behind the weaknesses which had an historical origin we are now beginning to see the weaknesses of human nature which were previously hidden by the others, and we see them as incurable. "Anthropological disappointment" is setting in.

Before the revolution, the socialist was confident that it meant the creation of a more human society—now he discovers bitterly that what he genuinely committed himself to was no more than the setting up of a "new class". His was not the final battle which will lead from prehistory into history.

This mood, so widespread today, could be given a name taken also from Walter Benjamin's work, "left-wing melancholy".[13] Benjamin uses it as the title for a review of some poems by Erich Kästner. It seems, however, to be an elliptical expression, in that Benjamin shortened a phrase from one of his own letters, "a left-winger's melancholy about the left", and later used it cryptically in a slightly different sense for the review.

Just as socialism is a universalist descendant of messianism, Zionism is its particularist descendant. Just as socialism looked forward to a new society, Zionism looked forward to a new nation; to this extent, in spite of all their historical conflicts,

[11] Manifesto of the Workers' Opposition, 1921.

[12] *Kursbuch* 30 (1972). I also owe these references, as well as one to Franz Pfemfert, who tried to combine expressionism and left-wing communism around 1920 in "Die Aktion" and was expelled from the German Communist Party, to Ernst Erdös.

[13] In "Angelus Novus", *Ausgewählte Schriften* 2 (Frankfurt, 1966); cf. the excursus on melancholy in Benjamin's book on tragedy (*Schriften* I, p. 271).

they have the same structure. Today Zionism, like socialism, has reached its goal, or at least the first stage of it, and for this reason, simultaneously with socialism, it is entering a related crisis. Becoming a nation or becoming a nation again could be a goal as long as it was still a new discovery, as long as the nation was threatened, had still to be founded or given an identity. But to make being a nation, once this could be taken for granted, the content of politics and life would be anachronistic, perverse and a distraction from new problems, the human and political problems of our age as a whole, the problem of nationality itself. The weakness of Zionism in our time is that it has still to learn how to live by what until now it lived for as a future.

Periods which include as part of their self-image the ideology of having progressed are worse than those which, lacking such a theory of history, simply accept themselves as they are. To disguise disappointment with the fulfilment they make it a dogma that fulfilment has been achieved, but this filter only makes reality seem to be controlled by malign powers. In such situations melancholy acts as a form of opposition. Even if it only takes the form of withdrawal it is nevertheless labelled as opposition by the propagandists of the *status quo* and condemned. In Campanella's *Utopie der Ordnung*, in which the norms of the system have to be strictly internalized, there are legal restrictions on melancholy, a prohibition of melancholy, as if in some early version of *Nineteen Eighty-Four*.[14] Among Campanella's successors today is Wolf Lepennies with his book *Melancholie und Gesellschaft*.[15] For any dominant ideology the disillusioned are more dangerous opponents than those who were never adherents, and it therefore tries to suggest that they are not disappointed.

With this basis in phenomena, let us turn to interpretation.[16] While fulfilment still lies ahead of us, we screw up our energies

[14] From Ernst Bloch, *Das Prinzip Hoffnung*, p. 39.
[15] His chapter on Robert Burton includes a history of the condemnation of melancholy (pp. 37 ff.); cf. pp. 90 ff.
[16] See M. Landmann, "Das Zeitalter der Erfüllungen", in *Des Ende des Individuums*; "Suchen und Haben", in *Erkenntnis und Erlebnis* (Berlin, 1951); "Der Moment des Erreichens", in *Pluralität und Antinomie* (Munich, 1963).

in an effort to reach it. In the process we grow out of ourselves. Our hopes make fulfilment shine in pure light. To reach and enjoy the fulfilment becomes ultimate meaning. But if we get there, our tensed muscles are no longer used and become slack. We lose our challenge and our pace with our goal. It is as though we had lost a friend who had been a close companion. Life stagnates and atrophies. The idea has become earth and present, the object of our fantasies has become ordinary. Whereas meaning flowed from the distant and embattled goal, the question of meaning now returns to torment us. It can only be pacified by an effort towards a new goal.

Psychiatrists talk of "release depression". In success we are not only gainers; something valuable is broken at the same time. Our poorer self was also a chosen one. Out of the fullness of possession there arises, however paradoxical it may seem and however much it contradicts the meaning of life, regret for the grace of the not yet, an "envy for longing" (Nietzsche).

We can describe the situation in historical terms. Since the time of the great civilizations and the Greeks man has never ceased to find and test out forms, and the repertoire of forms is now exhausted. The human race is entering Cournot's "post-histoire", in which it can no longer produce anything basically new since everything has been anticipated in the "creative phase" of its history, which is now over. This means that we ourselves are deprived of the most precious power of man, creation. We have in a way been brought back into primitive times, when magic kept the existing order intact and allowed nothing new to emerge. Today every gift is indeed encouraged, but time is once again still because all the great possibilities have long ago been discovered. For primitive man, though, comparison with the time of movement was impossible and the immobility was a naïve one. We have known the movement and lost it, and with us the immobility is marked by sadness.

Again, in the moment of fulfilment we often become aware for the first time of a situation like the following. We constantly set goals for ourselves, and we must do this because human life is not just an organic unfolding or blossoming, but driven by intellect and will, which by their nature insist on reasons and motives. As a result, as long as we are aiming at the goal we are completely in its power. It is really important to us to get near to it and get hold of it. But once we set foot in the promised land it as though an illusion, which was only necessary until now, disappears. We now realize that the goal simply had the function of stimulating life to a particular activity and giving a direction for a stretch. The goal was merely a pretext to give life this intensity and shape. To reach it was only the surface goal, and hidden within this was the true goal, to start off a movement towards the outer goal and saturate it at every point with meaning.

This attitude which denies the importance of the whole movement of history as compared with the achievement of goals has always been rejected by historians. As of other things, so too "history is the whole." This was the reason for the young Herder's rejection of any teleological view of history. For Herder, history had no "goal". It may have periods of greatness, but no less in status than these are the early periods, which are more than a preparation for the greatness, and late ones, which are more than end and decay. This new attitude was also applied to the stages of human life, and resulted in the rediscovery of childhood as more than a preparation for later maturity. Life too is "the whole".

Part of the sadness of success is also that it unmasks what we have previously regarded as an absolute goal as no more than an apparent goal. We recognize that its only meaning was to set a process in motion, but in this moment of recognition the process is at an end. Anyone who has had this experience will count it as part of maturity not to exaggerate the importance of goals and to give correspondingly more importance to the process stage. Constantine Cavafy has created a symbol of this attitude in his poem "Ithaca". We often learn something else as well in the moment of success,[17] and that is that we have selected the wrong goal, or set our sights too low; we have striven merely for the "small happiness". Just as there is disappointment in failure to succeed, in such cases there can also be resignation and despair in success. What looked from a distance like happiness

[17] On this cf. Norbert Hinske, "Glück und Enttäuschung", in Herbert Kundle (ed.), *Anatomie des Glücks*; cf. also his *Todeserfahrung und Lebensentscheidung*.

shows itself from close to as only "a shadow of happiness" (Thomas Aquinas). However, this experience, painful as it may be, need not remain negative. It can also free a person from his fixed expectations and give him the chance to reorient himself towards more appropriate and more solid aims. Crisis stimulates reflection; it releases something. "The moment of disappointment is also the moment of freedom" (Norbert Hinske).

Sadness in success may also have a cause other than the fact that we wrongly selected the ingredients of happiness. It may be sadness for which there is no help, no cure. This takes us into a new dimension, in which a fundamental distance opens up between our aspirations and what is within our reach. In our desire there is an element of the infinite, compared with which even the highest fulfilment remains bound by the limitations of earth and inadequate. Under the test of reality it never displays the same purity with which it was imagined in anticipation. Here metaphysical sadness is added to accidental sadness.

In the hope for the kingdom of God the promise which this world cannot make good can be honoured by another world. It is God alone who can give the gift of his kingdom, but nevertheless human behaviour is always allowed at least an influence on the time. According to the Old Testament prophets the people can delay its appearance by their neglect of the Law. The Cabbala describes man by his righteousness gathering together the messianic sparks scattered about a world despairing of redemption and so hastening its restoration (Tikkum).[18] Christianity also has those who are "anxious for the end", who "urge on Christ". On the other side there are those who stress the infinite difference between the moral and the religious dimension. The coming of the kingdom may wait for us in history, but it is not simply part of its unfolding, not just its final linear perfection. Redemption is always a transitus, a leap. Augustine's argument with Pelagius about the relation between human action and divine grace includes an eschatological as well as a personal perspective.

Walter Benjamin, in his "Theologisch-politisches Fragment",[19]

[18] From Gershom Scholem, *Jüdische Mystik* (Frankfurt, 1957), p. 300.
[19] *Illuminationen* (Frankfurt, 1961), pp. 280 ff. (not included in the English edition of *Illuminations*). On this cf. Rolf Tiedemann, *Studien zur Philosophie Walter Benjamins* (Frankfürt, 1965), who compares

insists on this incommensurability of temporal and messianic categories, although in the theses on the philosophy of history (which
for this reason must come from a different period or at least a
different mood) he combines both indiscriminately ("put differently" is the relation in thesis XVII). Both the Jewish and the
Marxists now claim Benjamin totally for themselves, but his
greatness must have lain in his ability, shown in his letters, to
carry both within himself in constant tension and identity. It
may have been the messianic impulse that gave him in his political development his distance from the left, and it may also have
been the source of his "left-wing melancholy".

"The order of the profane," says Benjamin, "has to be based
on the idea of happiness." The profane is not inherently connected with messianic goals, indeed "free mankind's search for
happiness" pushes "in a different direction from that messianic
movement". It is only the Messiah who fulfils all the events of
history by "redeeming", "creating" this connection. But nevertheless "just as a force by its motion can help another force
moving along an opposite path, the profane order of the profane can assist the coming of the messianic kingdom." The
profane "which has grown to perfection and is being success-
fully fulfilled" is not a category of the kingdom, but an indicator
of "its faint approach". At the same time—seen metaphysically,
from the point of view of the whole, of the end—"all earthly
life seeks its destruction in happiness". If this interpretation of
Benjamin is correct, while as far as it is concerned it seeks only
happiness, earthly life is really seeking something beyond, its
own destruction, which is at the same time transformation into
a higher form of existence. "Only in happiness ... is it destined
to find" this exalting "destruction".

This tension between the messianic and the profane is absent
from Ernst Bloch's work. The messianic element, however, is
not absent, which prompts us to ask whether he thinks of it
also in profane terms, or thinks of the profane also in messianic
terms. Bloch says that we must never allow ourselves to be se-

---

Augustine's philosophy of history and mentions Adorno's parallel distinction between profane progress and saving history (Adorno, "Fort-
schritt", *Stichworte*, Frankfurt, 1969, p. 32).

duced by any given situation into accepting it as final. All things are still alive with unexploited possibilities, carry utopias in their blood, live in exile and long for the native land they have never seen. Within every reality there is something at work which has not yet become reality. "Essence—matter in its most highly determined state—has not yet appeared." "The great construction site of human and world matter is still open."[20]

This knowledge is based in part on the utopian extra, "hope", which has still to work itself out everywhere. If this extra disappeared, the result would inevitably be "withering sadness". But on the other hand this knowledge acts on what has already appeared, with a twofold effect. In the first place, even in every success it feels the absence of what has not yet manifested itself. It opposes the "optimists of the incarnation" and remains suspicious "of any realization which makes extravagant claims".[21] This is the origin of Ernst Bloch's preference for the naturally raw,[22] for the baroque and romantic "open style", for fragments, for Michelangelo's torsos. They still contain an element of defiance, a protest. Their unfinished state opens up a perspective on what is still unrealized. On the other hand, the classical "closed form" suggests perfection as something existing and so prevents a future higher perfection. In the second place, however, the need to see, simultaneously with what a thing already is, what it is not yet, brings a dark undertone into the hopeful optimism and aggressiveness of Bloch's thought. It is here that Bloch stamps ideas with the "melancholy of fulfilment",[23] with the "non-arrival in advent" and the "bitter residue" in every realization. "We would yearn for utopias in Arcadia" (Jean Paul). This reminds us again of Benjamin—even the most complete happiness is only a preliminary and must "perish" for the sake of a still higher blessedness.

Translated by Francis McDonagh

[20] *Das Prinzip Hoffnung*, pp. 221–3; *Das Materieproblem*, p. 478.
[21] *Das Prinzip Hoffnung*, p. 210.
[22] Cf. T. W. Adorno, "Henkel, Krug und frühe Erfahrung", in Siegfried Unself (ed.), *Ernst Bloch zu ehren* (Frankfurt, 1965).
[23] *Das Prinzip Hoffnung*, p. 343.

Eugen Biser

The Scales of the Spirit
Nietzsche's Battle with the Spirit of Gravity

FRIEDRICH NIETZSCHE's roots were firmly in the great tradition, a fact which can be demonstrated most clearly by his opposition to it,[1] but he is nevertheless one of the exceptional figures of intellectual history, to be compared with a small number of others such as Dante, Pascal, Hölderlin, Kierkegaard and Solo-viev.[2] He is an exception even as regards his relation to the history of his influence, which with him was an integral part of his self-clarification. It is not just that Nietzsche, as Karl Löwith noted, predicted with amazing accuracy the point at

[1] By means of a detailed comparison of themes, my book on Nietzsche shows this interweaving of ideas in Nietzsche's rejection of God: Eugen Biser, 'Gott is tot'—Nietzsches Destruktion des christlichen Bewusstseins (Munich, 1962), pp. 36–62.

[2] There is a first attempt at a structural comparison of Nietzsche and Dante in my essay "Between Inferno and Purgatorio" in a forthcoming American symposium. There is as yet no comparison of Nietzsche and Pascal such as Josef Bernhart made with Meister Eckhart. The parallels between Nietzsche and Hölderlin were noticed by contemporaries; on this see E. Bertram, Nietzsche. Versuch einer Mythologie (Berlin, 1919), pp. 282 ff. Attention was drawn to the astonishing correspondences in the lives of Nietzsche and Kierkegaard by Karl Jaspers in "The Origin of the Contemporary Philosophical Situation", Reason and Existence (London, 1965), pp. 15–50; see also G.-G. Grau, "Nietzsche und Kierkegaard. Wiederholung einer unzeitgemässen Betrachtung", Nietzsche-Studien I (Berlin/New York, 1972), pp. 297–333. My book on Nietzsche (pp. 267 ff.) contains a brief comparison between Nietzsche and his Russian critic Soloviev, following Leo Shestov's description of Nietzsche and Dostoievsky as "twins" in a comparative study (1924). Finally in this list of comparisons comes Franz Brentano's sketch, "Nietzsche als Nachahmer Jesu", in Alfred Kastil (ed.), Die Lehre Jesu und ihre bleibende Bedeutung (Leipzig, 1922), pp. 129–32.

which his influence would begin its long-delayed growth;[3] he also foresaw the striking correspondence between the intellectual mood of various periods and his intellectual legacy. This is a fact, and shows itself in constantly new and often surprising associations. What seemed at one point to be finished, definitively overtaken by the process of development, at another unexpectedly acquires new relevance. What was thought to have been refuted seems in another context to be worth discussing. It is an advantage in these circumstances that Nietzsche was never able, in spite of constant efforts, to order his ideas into a system,[4] so that, even in the loosely connected form of the writings on the history of culture which preceded *Zarathustra*, they achieve their effect more through individual statements than through the combinations and deductions produced by ordering and linking. The effect is produced, to use an image from *Zarathustra*, by ideas which "flicker on high masts like a small flame—a small light indeed, yet a great comfort to sailors driven from their course, and to shipwrecked folk".[5]

The result is that more of his ideas are available than are at any time active, and this stock waits to be summoned by questions arising out of the changing patterns of intellectual interests and put into contemporary service.

In contrast to the recent past, the ideas "in demand" in this dialogue today are not the catchy phrases like "superman", "the death of God", "reversal of values" and "will to power", but comparatively "quiet" themes which have to do more with intellectual mood. This approach began with Martin Buber's discussion of the relation between religion and philosophy, published under the title *Gottesfinsternis* in 1953, which went back to Nietzsche's reference to the "period of gloom and eclipse, the like of which has probably never taken place on earth before,"[6]

---

[3] K. Löwith, "Nietzsche", in *Zeitgemässes und Unzeitgemässes* (Frankfurt, 1956), pp. 7–25.
[4] There is interesting new information about these efforts in Erich F. Podach, *Ein Blick in Notizbücher Nietzsches* (Heidelberg, 1963), pp. 13–108, 128–59.
[5] *Zarathustra* III, "Of the Spirit of Gravity", § 2. Quotations from *Zarathustra* are taken from the Everyman edition (rev. ed., London, 1957). Quotations from other works are from the edition of Nietzsche's collected works edited by Oscar Levy, London, 1909–1913.
[6] *The Joyful Wisdom* V, § 343.

which followed the death of God. In this context a religious variant of existentialism was offered as an answer to the madman's question: "Is there still an above and below? Do we not stray as through infinite nothingness? Does not empty space breathe on us? Has it not become colder? Does not night come on continually, darker and darker?"[7]

In the same category as these pointers to a diagnosis of the atmospheric state of his mind belong Nietzsche's repeated attempts to exorcize his "gravity" and the threat it presented to him. The euphoria and experience of an assistance in the literal sense inspirational which, at least in the retrospect of *Ecce Homo*,[8] accompanied the creation of *Zarathustra* make it natural that we should find the most important evidence on this point in this book, and especially in the chapter "On the Spirit of Gravity" in Part Three. Because of the poetic language of *Zarathustra* the various references cannot be simply added together to form a general diagnosis, and this is also ruled out by the "atmospheric" character of the subject. The "Spirit of Gravity" cannot be reduced to a definition or a precise concept, all the more so since, as will be seen, it is the basis of concepts and norms. The only way to obtain a more precise idea is to follow the trail of the most important references and descriptions.

I. THE SIGNATURE

The first and almost unavoidable question is what brought Nietzsche into contact with the issues summed up under the phrase the "Spirit of Gravity". An answer would have to take account of two features. First there is the young Nietzsche's strong sense of the conflict of existence; in his early essay "Fate and History", of 1862, he describes the teleology of spirit realizing itself in history as opposed by the blind necessity of fate. There is also a remark by his sister in a letter, which Nietzsche interpreted as both a confirmation and a challenge: "Truth is always on the side of seriousness."[9] Since the relevant statements are almost all in *Zarathustra*, however, a final answer must be

---

[7] *The Joyful Wisdom* III, § 125.
[8] *Ecce Homo*, "Why I write such excellent books: 'Thus spake Zarathustra' ".
[9] See his reply (June 1865).

looked for here. *Zarathustra* too is dominated by the sense of conflict which regards life as irreparably in conflict with itself and pushes towards simple syntheses. This is already hinted at in the idea of the domination of the "little intelligence" of the mind by the "great" intelligence of the unconscious powers of the body, the "prompter of concepts", which reaches its goals amid the "leaps and flights of thought".[10] It is this split within the life pressing towards truth which makes the path of knowledge, apparently so easy and covered in leaps and flights, seem a "way of affliction".[11] This initial position can be seen in its full sharpness in a passage from the chapter "Of Famous Wise Men" in Part Two: "Mind is that life which cutteth into life: by its own pain it increaseth its own knowledge. – Knew ye this already?

"And the mind's happiness is this: to be anointed and consecrated by tears as a sacrificial victim. – Knew ye this already?

". . . Ye know only the sparks of the mind: but ye see not that it is an anvil, nor see ye the cruelty of its hammer!"

Alongside this line of thought, which seeks a synthesis, even if an incomplete one, there is, as has been mentioned, a second line, of radical division and polarization. If we trace it back to its starting-point, we find that it is connected with the experience of initiation which produced the poetry of *Zarathustra*. In the autobiographical account of *Ecce Homo*,[12] which already shows clear traces of euphoria, Nietzsche, in what Thomas Mann called a "stylistic masterpiece", describes the creation of the work as an experience of volcanic release, as a task involving no effort, borne along by the pressure of images which pushed themselves forward in inexhaustible abundance and of a language which practically spoke itself. Mann says that this description is "comparable only to the marvellous analysis of the prelude to the *Meistersinger in Beyond Good and Evil* and to the Dionysiac description of the cosmos at the end of *The Will to Power*.[13]

[10] *Zarathustra* I, "Of the Despisers of the Body".
[11] *Zarathustra* I, "Of the Way of a Creator".
[12] See M. Montinari, "Ein neuer Abschnitt in Nietzsche's 'Ecce homo' ", *Nietzsche-Studien* I (1972), pp. 380–418.
[13] Thomas Mann, "Nietzsche's Philosophy in the Light of Recent History", *Last Essays* (London, 1959), p. 147.

Starting from the suggestive question, "Has anyone at the end
of the nineteenth century a conception of what the poets of
strong ages called inspiration?", Nietzsche, according to Thomas
Mann, gives "a description of illuminations, ecstasies, elations,
exaltations, feelings of divine power, which he takes as something
atavistic daemonically derivative from other, 'stronger' states
when man stood closer to the gods, states of being utterly exceptional, lifted far above the psychic possibilities of our feeble,
rational epoch." But at the same time what he was describing
was only "a dangerous condition of over-stimulation which
ironically precedes tertiary-luetic collapse."[14] The most important
feature of the decision involved in this original experience is not,
however, as Mann rightly emphasizes, the fact that it points to
luetic paralysis, but the feeling of an exceptional lightness of
speech and linguistic form, which accompanied the experience
of inspiration. This feeling made Nietzsche see the factor of
effort and gravity, as no longer an opposite pole to be taken into
account, but as an opponent to be conquered. It is only against
this background that it is possible to understand passages like
the following: "And when I beheld my devil, I found him
earnest, thorough, profound, solemn: he was the Spirit of Gravity—by him all things fall."[15] "I am God's advocate before the
devil: who himself is the Spirit of Gravity."[16] "Upwards—in
that spirit's despite that drew it downwards, abysswards—that
Spirit of Gravity, my devil and arch-enemy."[17]

In a similar mood is the appeal in which the first of these
passages ends, "One slayeth not by wrath but by laughter. Arise!
let us slay the Spirit of Gravity!"[18]

The reason for this intensification becomes apparent in the
chapter "Of the Vision and the Riddle", in which the Spirit of
Gravity becomes visible as a gnomelike form on Zarathustra's
back and, more depressingly, is perceived when he pours into
Zarathustra's mind the "leaden idea" that he too is inescapably
under the Spirit's law: "O Zarathustra, thou stone of wisdom,

[14] Thomas Mann, *ibid.*, p. 148.
[15] *Zarathustra* I, "Of Reading and Writing".
[16] *Zarathustra* II, "The Dance-Song".
[17] *Zarathustra* III, "Of the Vision and the Riddle".
[18] *Zarathustra* I, "Of Reading and Writing".

thou sling-stone, thou star-destroyer!—thou hast thrown thyself very high—but every stone that is thrown must fall!

"Condemned to thyself and thine own stoning: O Zarathustra, far indeed hast thou thrown the stone—but upon *thee* shall it fall!"[19]

Now the situation narrows for Zarathustra into the alternative "you or me?". The only other place where we find this is in the protest of the murderer of God, proclaimed the "ugliest man", against the all-seeing witness: "He ever saw me: on such a witness I would be revenged—or else not live at all!

"The God that saw all—*even man*—that God could not but die. Man could not *endure* that such a Witness should live."[20]

The correspondence is not accidental. The effect of both the look of the all-seeing witness and the gnome's suggestion is to cripple subjective initiative, to hold the "I" back from itself and its creative impulses. In Nietzsche's attack on the Christian idea of God what the "ugliest man" denounces as a crippling and instrusive gaze appears in the form of law morality, which fetters man in the shape of an external law. Similarly, in the chapter "Of Old and New Tables", Zarathustra calls the meeting-place of the gods, "where I found again mine ancient devil and arch-fiend, the Spirit of Gravity, and all his works—compulsion and dogma, necessity and consequence, purpose and will, good and evil."[21]

The return to the source can now be seen to have been anything but an unnecessary digression. It is not until we see the counter-position into which it led that we can fully appreciate the meaning of the signature we wanted to interpret. And even if we are still no nearer to a clear definition of the Spirit of Gravity, it is now clear at least what it mainly represented for Nietzsche. It is the "spirit" embodied in laws and norms, which by means of these forms imposes itself on human spontaneity as an alien law. This explains Zarathustra's answer to the objection "Life is hard to bear":

"But only man is hard for himself to bear. That is because

---

[19] *Zarathustra* III, "Of the Vision and the Riddle".
[20] *Zarathustra* IV, "The Ugliest Man".
[21] *Zarathustra* III, "Of Old and New Tables", § 2.

he carries too many alien burdens. Like the camel he kneels down and lets himself be heavily laden.

"Especially the strong man who can bear burdens—he is possessed by reverence. He lets himself be burdened with too many heavy words and values—now he feels life to be a desert."[22]

II. THE ANTITHESIS

The great inspirational experience in which, as *Ecce Homo* puts it, Zarathustra "seized" his poet as a type and, according to the same source, lifted him clear of all the obstacles to creation, has the result that for Nietzsche at first his opponent, the Spirit of Gravity, appeared in opposition to the body. This required only a slight rearrangement of what he had experienced. This is clearest in the passage from *Zarathustra* in which he depicts the exhilarating unity of freedom and necessity which dominated his creative process: "Here all things come fondling to thy speech and flatter thee: for they desire to ride on thy back. Here thou mayst ride on every parable to truth.

"... Here the words and word-shrines of being open suddenly unto thee: here all being desireth to become speech, all Becoming desireth to learn speech of thee."[23]

A sign that the rearrangement has been completed is the "Dance-Song" in which Zarathustra explains his delight at the maidens dancing in a glade: "I am God's advocate before the devil: who himself is the Spirit of Gravity."[24]

This delight in dancing corresponds to Nietzsche's striving to surmount the difficulties that face him and go on his way on the wings of the dance: "In the dance alone can I speak a parable of highest things."[25] Anyone who has the weariness of the climb behind him and has the longed-for peaks directly before him feels compelled to dance: "he that draweth nigh to his goal danceth."[26] The dance, therefore, is both the sign and the expression of imminent perfection. For Zarathustra, therefore, a

[22] *Zarathustra* III, "Of the Spirit of Gravity", § 2 (translation adapted).
[23] *Zarathustra* III, "Home-Coming".
[24] *Zarathustra* II, "The Dance-Song".
[25] *Zarathustra* II, "The Grave-Song".
[26] *Zarathustra* IV, "Of Higher Man".

God of norms and laws, a God, that is, in bondage to the "Spirit of Gravity", is a contradiction in himself. Such a God, it might be said, modifying the "last pope's" attack on God, is brought down by his excessive gravity. Hence Zarathustra's saying that he would believe "only in a god that knew how to dance".[27]

The remark is too much of an aside to be built into an image of a "dancing god", but this image is nevertheless so close that it appears as Nietzsche's antithesis to the God he sees as the essence of norms. In a comparison of themes, it appears in close contact with the "new ideal" which guides and goes on before the "Argonauts" of the exploration of the world without God mentioned at the end of *The Joyful Wisdom*:

> Another ideal runs on before us, a strange, tempting ideal, full of danger, to which we should not like to persuade anyone, because we do not so readily acknowledge anyone's *right thereto*: the ideal of a spirit who plays naïvely (that is to say involuntarily and from overflowing abundance and power) with everything that has hitherto been called holy, good, inviolable, divine; to whom the loftiest conception which the people have reasonably made their measure of value would already imply danger, ruin, abasement, or at least relaxation, blindness or a temporary self-forgetfulness; the ideal of a humanly superhuman welfare and benevolence; which may often enough appear *inhuman*, when put by the side of all past seriousness on earth, and in comparison with all past solemnities in bearing, word, tone, look, morality and pursuit, as their truest involuntary parody,—but with which, nevertheless, perhaps *the great seriousness* only commences, the proper interrogation mark is set up, the fate of the soul changes, the hour-hand moves, and tragedy begins.[28]

Here again the seductive dancing movement of the ideal is an anticipation of the perfection approached in daring confidence, a perfection brought within range by a break with everything previously regarded as good, valid and perfect. With the autonomy of the dance there goes the playful attitude to old laws, values and standards, which are cut from their eternal moorings and lose all their stability. Conversely, the disappearance of normative validity explains the lightness which characterizes all

[27] *Zarathustra* I, "Of Reading and Writing".
[28] *The Joyful Wisdom* V, § 382.

activity in the region beyond God. Dancing is the elementary reaction to the great release which existence experienced at the "death of God". In an unmistakable play on the words of the liturgy, Zarathustra, the messenger of life relieved of God, exhorts his followers: "Lift up your hearts, my brethren, high and higher. Neither forget your legs! Lift up your legs also, ye good dancers—and better yet if ye can stand upon your heads!"[29]

In this luxuriant imagery Zarathustra comes back to a type created by Nietzsche considerably earlier, which he characterized as "the free spirit". Seen in the context of his thought as whole, the free spirit is one of the types he constructed on his first venture into the no-man's-land lying beyond God as a sort of way-mark to help him survey the "new desert" with which he found himself faced.[30] This "free spirit" is "free" in the sense of released from all moorings and ties because he accepts the libertine principle, "Nothing is true, everything is allowed."[31] It acquires this attitude from its origin, intention and goal. The origin of the "free spirit" is in the "great emancipation", which is understood as absolute self-determination and freedom to choose one's own values,[32] and is ultimately freedom from a divinely ordered system. Its intention is directed towards unmasking philosophy as a "nihilistic movement",[33] and destroying the validity of morality.[34] In contrast to these, the goal of the "free spirit" consists in an act of self-transcendence by which the "free spirit" will be overtaken by "an even higher and more rebellious type" than even it represents.[35] This is causally connected with the "free spirit's" self-realization in the dance. The dance is dominated by the playful freedom of one from whom the heavy weights have fallen away and who has overcome the gravity which was pulling him downwards. But the dance Nietzsche is talking about is one of unrest. It is the unrest of the person who is compelled to keep on proving his freedom by

[29] *Zarathustra* IV, "Of Higher Man".
[30] *The Will to Power* § 617.
[31] *The Genealogy of Morals* III, § 24.
[32] 1886 Foreword to *Human, All-too Human*, § 3.
[33] From the title of the second book of the plan for re-ordering values (Autumn 1888).
[34] *Die Unschuld des Werdens* I, § 1112.
[35] *Die Unschuld des Werdens* I, § 1239.

constant changes of position. He is compelled to do this because he only possesses freedom as a reaction, as a revulsion from a previous state of moral or religious obedience. It is not surprising that the last leap of the dancing free spirit takes him out of himself. But where does it take him?

III. The Alternative

Since all movement finally gives way to a state of rest, the type in which the "free spirit" is to be transcended is characterized by rest and contentment. This appears fairly clearly in the verses which precede the chapter "Of the Spirit of Gravity". These refer to the "cowards and world-weary ones and spiders of the Cross", to whom Zarathustra holds out the following prospect: "And upon all these the day now cometh, the change, the sword of judgement, *the Great Noon*: then shall much be revealed!

"And he that proclaimeth the *I* to be wholesome and holy, and selfishness blessed, verily he proclaimeth that he knoweth— '*Behold, it cometh, it is nigh the Great Noon!*' "[36]

In connection with the interpretation of Nietzsche's "Great Noon", especially in *Zarathustra*, Karl Schlechta, in his monograph of the same name, has drawn attention to the play on biblical themes which runs through it, often in the form of parody.[37] Together with the apotheosis of Noon at the end of Hölderlin's "Hyperion", the world of Christian symbols is the most important background. This applies even more strongly to general Christian expectations of the end than to individual themes, so much so that it is hardly too much to call Nietzsche's noon an eschatology brought back into the present. As Zarathustra cries in his noon, "What? Is not the world even now grown perfect? Round and ripe? O round gold ring—whither doth it fly?"[38]

This is the Christian conception of the perfection of the world at the end of time, and the peace of fulfilment that goes with it, contracted into the timeless moment of darkening consciousness

[36] *Zarathustra* III, "Of the Three Evils", § 2.
[37] K. Schlechta, *Nietzsches grosser Mittag* (Frankfurt, 1954).
[38] *Zarathustra* IV, "At Noontide".

and stilled longing. Hyperion's experience of Diotima's return and the accompanying reconciliation in the disharmony of the universe was similar: "The discords of the world are like lovers' quarrels. Disputes contain reconciliation and everything that is separated is reunited. The veins in the heart part and unite, and there is nothing but a single, eternal, glowing life."

Here, as in Nietzsche, the world forms itself into the perfection of the circle, linking beginning and goal, and the heart, harnessed between the two, finds, if only for a timeless moment, reconciliation with itself and the world.

There can be no doubt that the freeing of existence which Nietzsche strove for is not achieved until this point. This means that it is only here that we can really talk of victory over the "Spirit of Gravity". This puts this victory in a new context, which for the first time makes all the connections clear. The explicit transition to this context comes in Zarathustra's antithetical critique of the "Spirit of Gravity":

"But only man is hard for himself to bear! That is because he carries too many alien burdens. Like the camel he kneels down and lets himself be heavily laden.

"Especially the strong man who can bear burdens—he is possessed by reverence. He lets himself be burdened with too many heavy words and values—now he feels life to be a desert.[39]

As the image of the kneeling camel shows, this passage is closely related to the doctrine of the three metamorphoses of the spirit which Zarathustra expounds at the beginning of his "discourses". The basic idea is announced in a style recalling the beginning of a prophecy: "I declare unto you three metamorphoses of the spirit: how the spirit became a Camel, the Camel a Lion, and the Lion at length a Child."[40]

Karl Löwith has done more than anyone else to bring out the meaning of this theme of metamorphosis. The first "metamorphosis", or, as Nietzsche says at a later stage of his thought, the first "course" of the spirit is its voluntary submission to the "yoke" of the values and norms which impose themselves on it.

[39] *Zarathustra* III, "Of the Spirit of Gravity", § 2 (translation adapted).
[40] *Zarathustra* I, "Of the Three Metamorphoses". There are theoretical reflections on the idea in the posthumous works *The Will to Power*, § 940, and *Die Unschuld des Werdens* I, § 662.

THE SCALES OF THE SPIRIT 57

Through this it achieves a first, but completely inadequate, adjustment of self and world, which it carries with it throughout its life as an alien burden like Sisyphus' stone. Zarathustra confirms this when—perhaps in a play on the dragon scene in Wagner's *Siegfried*—talks about the great dragon called "Thou shalt" which stands in the way of the human spirit in its search for full and unimpaired selfhood:

" 'Thou shalt' lies gold-glittering in his path, a scaly beast: on each scale there shineth in letters of gold: 'Thou shalt'.

"Thousand-year-old values shine on those scales, and thus says the mightiest of all Dragons: 'all value in all things shineth in me.' "[41]

The unhappiness of this stage consists, as Zarathustra's image implies, in the fact that man stays in it. Within the externality of "Thou shalt" is a deep inner urge to be negated in the autonomy of the "I will". The path of the strong spirit leads into the desert: "But in the solitude of the desert there comes the second metamorphosis: there the spirit becometh a Lion, that seeketh to seize freedom as his prey and to be lord in his own desert."[42] In a later part of the discourse Zarathustra explains being "lord" as freedom for creative activity:

"To create new values—even the Lion is not able to do this: but to create for himself freedom for new creation, for this the Lion's strength is sufficient.

"To create for himself freedom and an holy *Nay* even to duty; therefor, my brethren, is there need of the Lion."[43]

The connection with the type of the "free spirit" is so clear that it needs no demonstration. Conversely, the qualification that the new stage brings freedom for new creation, but not freedom to create new values, highlights even more sharply than before the limits by which the free spirit's freedom is bounded. It is, as Zarathustra says elsewhere, freedom from, not freedom for, in other words, freedom which is exhausted in acts of separation and self-assertion.[44] This gives meaning and justification to the third stage. Zarathustra asks, "Tell me what the Child can do which even the Lion could not." He gives the answer himself:

[41] *Ibid.*   [42] *Ibid.*   [43] *Ibid.*
[44] *Zarathustra* I, "Of the Way of a Creator".

"The Child is innocence and oblivion, a new beginning, play, a self-rolling wheel, a primal motion, an holy yea-saying."[45]

In the stage of the Child the compulsion to keep on proving oneself free is transcended in the peace of actual, unself-conscious freedom. The peace is such that the reaching of the goal is experienced as a totally new beginning. "New beginning" here means something like totally at one with oneself and so relieved of the burden of having to win freedom by proving oneself. Those who have reached this stage have acquired peace with themselves and the world. For them, as in Zarathustra's noon, the world has become "round and ripe". They have no questions to put to it and in turn are not exposed to its questions. The pressure of problems has given way before them; the desires of their souls have been stilled. The relief which they enjoy as a result is the real alternative to the burden imposed by the Spirit of Gravity. In view of the strong influence of Christian themes, among which here, hardly disguised, divine sonship appears in the image of the Child, it could even be said that the third stage brings "redemption" from the Spirit of Gravity, whom Zarathustra once calls, in biblical language, and significantly in the context, the "Lord of the world".[46]

Seen in the total context, Nietzsche's resolve to overcome the Spirit of Gravity only achieves its purpose in the figure of the Child, in other words in the I-am, which has consumed the labour of the "Thou shalt" in itself in its battle with the I-will. The antithesis of the dance was an inadequate expression of this. The unrest of the dance is not yet the counter-position to the sphere of heteronomy with its fear and reverence, imposition and rejection of values. The counter-position is not reached except in childlike play, which is goal and satisfaction in itself. The situation in this highest stage, denoted by the Child, is like that in a game, which follows its course without any of the players being able to control it. It is not the result of predeter-

---

[45] Schlechta, *Nietzsches grosser Mittag*.
[46] *Zarathustra* II, "The Dance-Song". The fourth gospel has Jesus' famous saying, with reference to his approaching death, "Now shall the ruler of this world be cast out" (Jn. 12. 31), and Paul says that "the god of this world has blinded the minds of the unbelievers" (2 Cor. 4. 4).

THE SCALES OF THE SPIRIT 59

mined processes or deliberate actions, but the product of an ultimate favour which bestows itself. Only this stage carries the seal of perfection by which all human efforts are measured because it is impressed with it from within.

IV. RELEVANCE

The close interweaving of themes, particularly around the alternative, presents the Christian theologian with a challenge to follow up the underlying polemical implications and draw his own conclusions. The resulting task divides into two main questions. Firstly, what in particular is the object of the criticism contained in the title "Spirit of Gravity"? Secondly, how can a Christian self-criticism take account of it?

The answer to the question of fact can start, appropriately, with a remark made by Zarathustra himself. He says that the main forms in which the Spirit of Gravity is embodied and can be experienced by anyone are "compulsion and dogma, necessity and consequence, purpose and will, good and evil". This, however, taken in connection with Nietzsche's overall strategy, is the Christian moral teaching which Nietzsche constantly attacks with the utmost vehemence, but now only in the light which, with other perspectives, follows from the "atmospheric" categories. The targets of Nietzsche's polemic are not moral values, laws and norms in their role as the embodiment of a divine will in opposition to autonomous human will, but these values and norms in their restrictive and repressive action on a human will which demands free development. There can be no doubt at all that Christian morality, like any other form of morality, is in constant danger of being misinterpreted in this way and, as a result of this misinterpretation, of being translated into a repressive system. The main support for this claim comes from Jesus himself, who made a similar charge against the "scribes" belonging to the caste of the Pharisees: "They bind heavy burdens, hard to bear, and lay them on men's shoulders; but they themselves will not lift a finger to help them carry the burdens" (Mt. 23. 4).

Attacking this evil spirit of slavery, which surrounds the whole of life with a fine mesh of petty regulations, Paul begs, "If with

Christ you died to the elemental spirits of the universe, why do you live as if you still belonged to the world? Why do you submit to regulations? 'Do not handle, Do not taste, Do not touch." (Col. 2. 20–21). These two passages themselves show that the Spirit of Gravity is not unknown to Christianity. If we go on to assume that the tendency attacked by Jesus and Paul in these polemics subsequently became stronger and, particularly after the Church's entry into the sphere of political and ideological powers, developed into a highly stable and extremely efficient system of repression, we may even come to feel that it has constantly accompanied the development of Christianity like a steadily growing shadow. To complete this impression it is enough to see that the shadow still spreads its chilling and crippling influence over Christian thought and action. In spite of the loosening of the pressure of normative attitudes as a system through the growth of partial areas of freedom, the sense of oppression it creates continues to act in the "atmosphere", in the form of psychological trends, suggestive tendencies and neurotic restrictions. The main factor long ago ceased to be the pressure to perform certain actions attacked by Luther as "righteousness by works", but this has been replaced by repressive factors of a quite different sort. Among these, psychotic fixations, disguised as dogmatic positions, are steadily increasing in importance. The operation of the mechanism is relatively easy to see. As hierarchical structures lost their force, their previous control functions were taken over by anonymous "authorities", which mostly took the form of élite groups. In areas controlled, even partially, by these groups very little real dialogue could ever start. Even when disputes take on the appearance of a meeting and exchange of ideas, on closer inspection they prove to be more than tactical struggles. Where the Spirit of Gravity takes over, the minimum of spiritual freedom and mobility required for a resolution of conflicts through dialogue is absent.

The fact that it is even possible to consider overcoming these pressures within Christianity is connected with the stage of thought reached by Christian awareness. In the examination of the problem the understanding of its origin and of the operation of the mechanisms responsible for the constricting pressure gradually changed. This itself has already produced one possible form of resistance, an attempt to produce one possible form of resistance, an attempt to produce a thorough analysis of the sources of the pressures which cripple initiative and of the origin of psychotic restrictions on awareness. The factors thus revealed include both the continuing effects of historical features and completely new causes. Of particular importance in addition to the familiar pressures of the system are the previously unrecognized signs of weariness produced in many people by the attempt to identify with the existing Church forms. Analysis of causes, however, is not enough. Equally important is a functional analysis of the crippling mechanisms, since only through this can we learn how to stop them. The findings of modern ethology and group psychology are of considerable value here.

The final answer, however, is provided not by analysis, but by the Christian gospel itself. It is so familiar that it hardly requires explicit mention. The figure of the Child in the discourse about the three metamorphoses contains in unmistakable form the Christian alternative, which the message of salvation talks about as divine sonship. The only obstacle to the explicit development of this alternative is the circumstance that theology has made only sporadic use of this theme, and hardly ever with the required intensity. A notable exception is Cusanus' "On divine sonship" (1445), which says of perfection in the next world: "I believe that we will not become children of God in the sense that we shall become something different from what we now are; rather, we shall be in a different mode and measure what we are now in a mode and measure appropriate to the present."[47]

Nicholas of Cusa sees the transition to this state as a progression from discipleship to mastery; for him growing to maturity as children of God means "working up to that mastery which is achieved in being a child".[48] Though very different in origin and intention, the idea is still amazingly close to Nietzsche's idea of the "free spirit" as the conqueror of Gravity. The necessary middle term is the idea of a sovereignty raised above normative rules, which Nicholas of Cusa sees as achieved by

[47] *De filiatione Dei,* folio 65v.
[48] *Ibid.* Among recent theologians the most important to have taken up the theme is Hermann Kuhaupt, *Die Formalursache der Gotteskindschaft* (Münster, 1940).

adaptation and mastery of the laws and Nietzsche by a mastery which breaks them in the same sense in which records are broken.

There can be no doubt that in this area there is a great deal of ground to be made up. Christian instruction nevertheless remains satisfied with instruction in the "first principles", which the Epistle to the Hebrews long ago said we should have got beyond: "For though by this time you ought to be teachers, you need someone to teach you again the first principles of God's word. You need milk, not solid food" (Heb. 5. 12). What is lacking in the Church as a whole as well as in the guardians of the magisterium is the (completely loyal) attitude of sovereignty to the content of tradition which alone makes possible its creative renewal. In principle this is not a matter of talent, but of the "mastery" which, in Nicholas of Cusa's interpretation at least, the divine sonship confers upon us. Related to the present situation of the faith, this means that to meet the Spirit of Gravity in all its different manifestations we need an attitude which consistently implements the principle of divine sonship. Only as children of God can we have, like the Child in Nietzsche's parable, that almost playful feeling for the world of faith which is remote from the gravity of the religion of law in the same way that that gravity makes everything it takes hold of remote from faith.

But even this answer is not the last word. In the Christian dispensation the final power does not belong to the operation of principles, but to him who is in his person the beginning and the source. After all the partial answers to the question of overcoming gravity have been given, the question is passed to him. Nor is he without an answer. He gives it in the same saying in which he offers himself to the oppressed and burdened as a helper and support: "Come to me, all who labour and are heavy laden, and I will give you rest. Take my yoke upon you, and learn from me; for I am gentle and lowly in heart, and you will find rest for your souls" (Mt. 11. 28–29).

In this saying Jesus does not simply release his followers from hardships and burdens—on the contrary, he says that he himself is laying a burden on them. But he calls his yoke and his burden light, because he joins his followers in bearing the weight. In other words, as the giver of his commandment he is also its first

THE SCALES OF THE SPIRIT 63

doer. He imposes nothing that he does not take upon himself. In this way his yoke joins us in a permanent sharing of life with him. So literally true is this that we have to ask which comes first. Does he come to our side so that we can bear his yoke, or is the yoke really his means of bringing us into fellowship with him? But whichever it is, Jesus wishes that men bowed under the burden of their lives and crushed by it in so many ways should be helped. Nor does he make this wish known just in word and deed; he even offers himself as helper and help.[49] In his company we are freed from the burden of existence. Thus in the last resort it is he himself, in the help he offers, who overcomes the Spirit of Gravity. When we rely on him we are entitled and enabled to encourage ourselves in the face of the facts which drag us down with the call *Sursum corda!*

Translated by Francis McDonagh

[49] For details see my book on Jesus, *Der Helfer. Eine Vergegenwärtigung Jesu* (Munich, 1973).

PART II
PRINCIPLES

Francis Fiorenza

Joy and Pain as Paradigmatic for Language about God

AN old story relates how a son had gone away from his father's house to visit foreign places. After travelling to many different places and after visiting various foreign countries, he returns home twenty years later. His father greets him with the question, "What have you learned from your long journey to such far away places and strange cultures?" The son replies, "I have learned that there is a God." The father calls his servants and asks each of them, "Does God exist?" Every single one of them replies, "Yes, of course, there is a God." Turning towards his son, the father reproachfully demands, "Why did you have to travel all over the earth and visit foreign cultures just to tell me what everyone else knows, what every servant of mine can tell me?" The son's reply is short and to the point. "Everyone may know it, but I have learned what it means that there is a God."

This story illustrates two surprising features of the contemporary German theological discussion about God. At a time when the possibility and meaning of language about God is in question, the translation of the work of a Japanese theologian[1] has occasioned a shift in the direction and thematic of the discussion of God. In applying a fundamentally Japanese understanding to the concept of God, he has given the impetus to a turn from questions of epistemology and semantics to questions of the nature and attributes of God. In addition, although much of what he writes is not new and is in fact part of the common

---

[1] K. Kitamori, *Theology of the Pain of God* (Richmond, 1965).

tradition of biblical and popular language about God, his book has been appealed to by theologians like Jürgen Moltmann[2] and Rudolf Weth[3] for teaching them something about God which they should have known from Luther.

I

Our understanding and our language about God involves epistemological, semantic, and metaphysical issues.[4] Although they do not involve completely separate questions and are intimately related to one another, for the sake of cataloguing recent discussion about God, they can be distinguished. The epistemological question has been with us since Immanuel Kant asked to what extent can man know what transcends experience. Is God knowable or is he only a transcendental ideal or an intellectual projection of unity for the universe? Attempts were made to answer these questions either by an appeal to religious experience as a dimension of man's total experience of reality or as a specific experience or by an appeal to the knowledge of God based only on his revelation through the authority of Scripture or Church. Both of these responses have been called into question in recent years. The "death of God" theologians have argued against the appeal of liberalism to a religious experience and against the appeal of neo-orthodoxy to a supernaturalistic revelation that contemporary man not only lacks an experience of God but also experiences the absence of God. Their critique of previous theological constructions has raised anew the epistemological problem of our knowledge of God.[5]

In addition, the semantic or linguistic issues have been very much in the fore of the theological discussion in Anglo-Saxon countries. The term "God" involves specific semantic and linguistic problems because it is a term which by definition has only a transcendent reference. It does not refer to a reality that is locat-

[2] Der gekreuzigte Gott. Das Kreuz Christi als Grund und Kritik christlicher Theologie (Munich, 1972).
[3] "Heil im gekreuzigten Gott," Evangelische Theologie, 31 (1971), pp. 227–43.
[4] G. D. Kaufmann, God: The Problem (Cambridge, Mass., 1972).
[5] L. Gilkey, Naming the Whirlwind: The Renewal of God-Language (New York, 1969).

able within human experience. The believer might profess that he experiences a deep feeling or an intense affection in his heart of God, but God is not to be identified with this emotion. The biblicist will suggest that God is to be found in the Bible where his word is revealed and the ethicist will believe that God speaks through men's consciences. But neither the biblicist nor the ethicist will assert that this locus adequately defines God. Each will assert that God transcends the locus that they appeal to in their affirmation of God. The problem of the meaning of our language about God is acute because if absolutely nothing within human experience can be directly and adequately the referent for our language what value does language about God have? Can language about God be meaningful when the word "God" has no adequate referent in our experience? Theories of the non-referential character of language may help us to understand the meaning of "God-language" but they leave the question of truth unresolved.[6]

The metaphysical problem has been raised by the theological movement known as "process theology". Influenced by the philosophy of Alfred North Whitehead, theologians such as Schubert Ogden,[7] John Cobb, Jr.,[8] and Daniel D. Williams[9] have challenged the classical conception of God. They attempt to develop the significance of a new metaphysic for the Christian faith because in their opinion the classical metaphysical tradition has failed to adequately conceive of a genuine relation between God and the world. For this classical tradition God has no real future, is in no way affected by the events of the world, and nothing is really new for him. He cannot suffer and cannot be subject to change in himself. This metaphysical understanding of God has in its neo-Platonic tradition influenced Anselm and Thomas as well as Calvin and Luther despite its apparent contradiction to the biblical image of an active passionate God. Consequently, the process theologians seek to develop a perspective in which God's Being and his relation to the world can be

---

[6] R. S. Heimbeck, *Theology and Meaning. A Critique of Metatheological Scepticism* (Standford, 1969).
[7] *The Reality of God* (New York, 1966).
[8] *A Christian Natural Theology* (Philadelphia, 1965).
[9] *God's Grace and Man's Hopes* (New York, 1965).

interpreted in terms of temporality, freedom, becoming, and suffering. These elements belong to all existence and should have their place as aspects of God's Being.[10] Strangely enough process theology has significant influence only in Anglo-Saxon countries and has been of little importance to contemporary German theological thinking despite the fact that a tradition of processual thought exists in the work of Hegel and Schelling[11] and despite Karl Barth's understanding of the nature of God's Being.[12]

II

In this situation, the appearance of Kazoh Kitamori's *Theology of the Pain of God* is of significance. Whereas its English translation has gone without notice, its German translation has had a catalytic effect. Writing as if the epistemological and semantic issues in the theological discussion about God did not exist, Kitamori argues that the essence of God is his pain and that Christians are called to serve the pain of God by their own pain. Like the process theologians he claims that the traditional Christian understanding of God has been unduly influenced by the conceptualization in Greek philosophy of the notions of substance and essence and has failed to do justice to the image of God presented by the prophets and by Paul. By concentrating on the essence of God, the Christian tradition has not taken into account the biblical references to the heart of God and has therefore not understood the true nature of God. Kitamori's specific contribution, however, consists in his suggestion that this heart of God is characterized by pain and should be understood from the analogy of the fundamental Japanese experience of "tsurasa". For the Japanese way of thinking a man of depth and of understanding is one who comprehends tsurasa. If a man is not sensitive to tsurasa, then he is not only shallow-minded and jejune but also not a true and genuine person.

What is, however, the nature of tsurasa? Kitamori explains it as the basic principle of Japanese tragedy that is realized when

---

[10] D. D. Williams, "Prozess–Theologie: Eine neue Möglichkeit für die Kirche," *Evangelische Theologie*, 30 (1970), pp. 571–82.

[11] W. Kasper, *Das Absolute in der Geschichte* (Mainz, 1965); J. Habermas, *Das Absolute und die Geschichte* (Bonn, 1954).

[12] E. Jüngel, *Gottes Sein ist im Werden* (Tübingen, 1964).

someone dies or makes his beloved son die for the sake of others. This pain in the sacrifice of one's beloved son for others constitutes the essence of tsurasa. This description of tsurasa illustrates the meaning of the pain of God. This pain is not just an effect of God's heart nor is it a mere act of God, but it constitutes God's deepest nature and the essence of his relation to others. The death of Jesus on the cross, consequently, is the revelation of God's true nature because through the cross we learn that God has suffered in sacrificing his son. From the cross we learn that the God of love who was proclaimed so vigorously by the liberal theology does not represent the Christian understanding of God because the God of liberalism is only a God of love who offers nothing but a "cheap love" and is without pain or wrath. God is instead a God of pain because he suffers in loving and his love is established through his suffering. This pain of God is so fundamental to the nature of God that Kitamori claims that even God's love is rooted in his pain.

Kitamori's theological concentration on the pain of God has found its resonance in Jürgen Moltmann's recent book, *The Crucified God*. Echoing many of Kitamori's suggestions for an adequately Christian understanding of God and for the interpretation of the significance of Jesus' death on the cross for God himself, Moltmann develops a theology of the cross which departs from the traditional approach. Whereas the latter concentrates on the soteriological meaning of Jesus' death and applies it to the justification of sinners, Moltmann reflects upon the significance of the suffering and death of Jesus for God himself. The theological tradition comprehended the death of Jesus in its salvific significance "for us" and saw the Christian preaching and the Eucharist as a making present and as a remembering of this salvation, but it did not ask what meaning Jesus' death had for God, whom Jesus called his father. Since Moltmann asserts that Jesus died not only for us, but also for God, he claims that his death on the cross, if rightly understood, involves a revolution in our understanding of God and demands that an authentically Christian understanding of God must be staurocentric. The death of Jesus is first of all and primarily a statement about God before it is a statement or promise of salvation to men. Just as Christian preaching of salvation is not possible without a new proclamation of God, so too the preaching of the cross of Jesus is only possible if it is the proclamation of a new understanding of the nature of God.

In the conceptuality of an incarnational view of Jesus Christ with its teaching of one person and two natures the death of Jesus is a human death and only in so far as God has assumed this human nature and by virtue of the *communicatio idiomatum realis* can one speak of the death of God. An important distinction, however, should be observed between speaking of "God in the Crucified" and speaking of "God on the cross". If Luther's statement is taken seriously that for the Christian faith God is not only in Jesus, but he is God himself, then, in Moltmann's opinion, it must be asserted that "what happened on the cross was an event between God and God; there God fights with God, there God cries after God, there God dies on God."[13] This event of Jesus' death on the cross is also an inter-trinitarian event and it raises the question of the suffering of God.

What the metaphysical tradition of neo-Platonism did not allow that is demanded by the event of the cross. The Christian God is not the apathetic God of the ancient Greek world, but is a suffering God. How does God suffer? How should we speak of the pain of God? Here Kitamori and Moltmann are very similar. The death of God the Son is for Kitamori the pain of God because the person of the Father lived and pain can be suffered only by the living. God the Father who hides himself in the death of the Son suffers pain because he still lives even in the death of his Son. The Son suffers a real death and the darkness of this death involves real pain. In short the pain of God is not only the pain of God the Son nor only the pain of God the Father but the pain of the two persons who are one God. Kitamori believes that his position is distinct from the Sabellian heresy of Patripassianism because this refers only to the sufferings of Jesus on earth. It does not comprehend the Trinitarian aspect of the pain of God, whereas his position demands that both Father and Son suffer pain.[14]

Moltmann takes as his starting-point the observation that what

[13] J. Moltmann, "Gesichtspunkte der Kreuzestheologie heute," *Evangelische Theologie*, 33 (1973), p. 351.
[14] *Op. cit.*, p. 115.

he did not abandon he allowed
he submitted

Abraham did not have to do to Isaac God the Father did with Jesus and abandoned him to the fate of death. The Father abandons and sacrifices his own Son. The Son experiences the curse, abandonment and handing over by the Father in his passion and death even though he had preached the grace of his Father.

NO

The Father suffers in the pain of his love the death of his Son. Because the suffering and pain of the Son differs from that of the Father, Moltmann likewise asserts that one cannot speak in a theopaschitic sense of God's death, but one can speak of a Patricompassianism. Moreover, Moltmann completes the Trinitarian interpretation of the death of Jesus on the cross by explaining that out of this event between the Father and the Son proceeds the Spirit. He makes the death alive; he justifies the godless; and he accepts the abandoned. In short, Moltmann asserts that the suffering and pain of this world is not an event external and outside of God, but an event within the Trinity itself so that the history of pain in the world is also a part of God's inner history.

III

When Kitamori and Moltmann call for a new understanding of God's nature, they are proposing a twofold revision. They are suggesting first of all that the classical metaphysical concept of God as apathetic be revised in consonance with biblical images of God and in fidelity to biblical statements about God. But they are also proposing a very specific revision in so far as they claim that the Christian God is a God who is in pain and suffers and in so far as they suggest a speculative understanding of the death of Jesus as an inter-trinitarian event. Yet what is the basis for their suggested understanding of God as God? It is the claim that the biblical image of God presents and contains such an understanding of God. But is this true?

Kitamori has searched the Scriptures for a biblical confirmation of his theology of the pain of God, of his explanation of the significance of Jesus' death on the cross. Only two references of significance were discovered: Jeremiah 31. 20 and Isaiah 63. 15. These two passages use the word *hāmadh* which can mean either "to sound" or the "condition of man's (or God's) heart." In those references that it refers to a man's heart, it means his heart is in pain, he moans, he is in turmoil and he is disquieted. Consequently, Kitamori suggests that for Jeremiah 31. 20, it should refer to God's pain. Both Luther's and Calvin's translation of the passage confirm this passage. Unfortunately, modern translations of the passage refer to God's yearning or the inner excitement of the heart of God and modern dictionaries tend to soften the meaning of the word to mean "sympathetic feeling". The use of the word *ḥāmadh* in Isaiah 63. 15 refers to God's love, or, more precisely, his compassion. Instead of taking this observation as a partial refutation of his thesis, Kitamori argues that *ḥāmadh* implies "pain" and "love" interchangeably or simultaneously. This usage is taken to confirm his thesis that God's love is founded in his pain and this is the central biblical message. Obviously such an exegetical foundation is very tenuous. To take one word that is applied to God twice in the Old Testament and has a broad spectrum of meanings and to claim that only one of those meanings is the correct and fundamental interpretation despite modern translations is to take a rather arbitrary approach to Scripture. The least that can be said is that such an exegetical foundation is inadequate to support his thesis.

More central to the foundation of their thesis, especially in the case of Moltmann, is the appeal to the New Testament and the death of Jesus on the cross. The claim that the death of Jesus entails a revolution and a revision of the classical Greek metaphysic idea of God entails a contradiction when it is based upon the New Testament. The distinction between the Father and Jesus is such that it would be unthinkable for a New Testament author that the suffering of Jesus would involve a suffering of the Father because of an identity of nature between Father and Son. It is precisely the Hellenistic metaphysical thinking with its concepts of substance and nature that maintain such an identification. To criticize Hellenistic metaphysical thinking while at the same time basing a presupposition of one's critique on the thought patterns of that very system is, to say the least, not consistent.

In short, it is questionable whether from an exegetical perspective it is legitimate to speak of the pain of God. Kitamori's one Old Testament reference is ambiguous. The appeal to the

New Testament and the death of Jesus on the cross can only allow an interpretation of the death of Jesus on the cross as an inter-trinitarian event, as an event in Moltmann's words of "God against God"[15] if one reads into the New Testament a heterogeneous speculative view of the Trinity. The variety of views within the New Testament of Jesus' relation to the Father and of the meaning of his death on the cross do not speak for a Trinitarian theology of the pain of God. Even those reflections that constitute a theology of the cross in the New Testament have to be seen as a later theologumon to understand the historical event of Jesus' death. These critical reflections, however, are made with the realization that the problems, questions and issues, which Kitamori and Moltmann have raised, are fundamental for our understanding of God and the Christian proclamation.[16] The metaphysical problem of the nature of God or of the possibility of a theology of the pain of God can only be adequately approached from the perspective of the epistemological and semantic problem, namely, the problem of the possibility of language about God and the meaning of such language. Unfortunately, neither Moltmann nor Kitamori has placed their metaphysical constructions of God who suffers and is in pain in such a context. In the following analysis, we should like to suggest what significance this context can have for the discussion of the pain of God.

IV

Any attempt to discuss the problem of the pain of God should be self-conscious of the linguistic horizon of reality. In discussing the pain of God, we must be aware that we are first of all dealing not with God directly but with a question of our language about God. Since all meaning is mediated through language, we must first ask what is the meaning of our language about

[15] Der gekreuzigte Gott, op. cit., pp. 145 f., cf. pp. 177–88, 233 f.
[16] H. Küng, Menschwerdung Gottes. Eine Einführung in Hegels theologisches Denken as Prolegomena zu einer künftigen Christologie (Freiburg, 1970); H. Urs von Balthasar, "Mysterium Paschale," in Mysterium Salutis, III, 2 (Einsiedeln, 1969); H. Mühlen, Die Veränderlichkeit Gottes als Horizont einer zukünftigen Christologie (Münster, 1969); fundamental to some of these authors are Karl Rahner's reflections on the Trinity and Incarnation in Theological Investigations, IV (London, 1964).

God before we can ask what is the meaning of statements about the pain of God. The metaphysical problem can only be approached when the epistemological and semantic issues have become clarified. This approach should begin with the question of the meaning of language.

A traditional position on the meaning of language is the referential or "word-object" theory of meaning. Having its historical legacy in Plato's *Cratylus* and in Augustine's *Confessions*, this referential theory of meaning presupposes that a word or an expression has a specific meaning if something exists to which the term or expression refers. For this reason Gilbert Ryle has labelled this view the "Fido-Fido" theory of meaning. It assumes that words transparently function as names just as the word "Fido" may refer to a specific object, namely, a specific dog.[17] In his *Philosophical Investigations* Ludwig Wittgenstein has argued that this referential theory does describe a system of communication, but it does not cover all that language entails. It does not give an adequate or satisfactory explanation of language and of how meaning is mediated through language. Whereas the referential theory does call attention to the significance of the reference that words do make, it overlooks that language contains meaningful expressions that do not have co-ordinate objects. Moreover, it misrepresents the referential function of language when it assumes that the connection between language and the world is a piecemeal correspondence between one thing (a word) and another thing (an object of the world). This misrepresentation leads to a conception of language in terms of abstract substantives and presupposes that meaning could be categorized independent of language as if the world was an entity made up of independently meaningful entities.[18]

The inverse counterpart of this referential theory of meaning is the "word-image" or "ideational theory". It also makes a

[17] "The Theory of Meaning," *British Philosophy at the Mid-Century*, ed. C. A. Mace (London, 1966).

[18] L. Wittgenstein, *Philosophical Investigations* (Oxford, 1958). It would be inaccurate to characterize Wittgenstein's argumentation as involving a complete denial of the referential character of words. For a good collection, see G. H. R. Parkinson (ed.), *The Theory of Meaning* (London, 1968); see also: L. J. Cohen, *The Diversity of Meaning* (London, 1962) and S. J. Schmidt, *Bedeutung und Begriff* (Brunswick, 1969).

referential assumption about language but instead of referring words to objects, it refers words to mental ideas or intellectual object. Language would then consist of symbols that refer to intellectual concepts and mental images and language would then be the attempt to communicate to others the mind's concepts and ideas. Words are considered vehicles, and inadequate ones at that, to convey meaning. They merely symbolize the thoughts or ideas, but it is only in the thoughts and ideas that words have their meaning. The inadequacy of such a theory becomes evident when we reflect that not only do we not have mental images of all words (e.g. "but," "however," etc.) but our images are also not necessarily self-evidently intelligible or meaningful. They can receive different applications and various interpretations. Our understanding and knowledge of the meaning of words consists of using them correctly in an intersubjective context.[19]

In criticizing these two theories, Wittgenstein is arguing against regarding every word as a name as if pseudo-entities served as the objects of reference for abstract nouns and against considering the understanding of the meaning of a word as involving a mental process which involves the contemplation of what Locke names an idea and Schlick called a content. When Wittgenstein suggests that words have their meaning primarily through their use and application, he does not mean that words receive their meaning from the individual's use of them as if meaning were private and esoteric but rather the contrary. The meaning of a word depends upon its public context and social usage.[20] With this emphasis upon the social character of meaning and with this affirmation of the linguistic character of meaning Wittgenstein has brought to Anglo-Saxon analytic tradition an understanding of meaning that shares common elements with the German hermeneutic position that has been developed under the influence of a Hegelian tradition. While these traditions might have different tendencies (e.g. the naturalistic tendency

[19] K. Apel, *Analytic Philosophy of Language and the Geisteswissenschaften* (Dordrecht, 1967).
[20] Cf. J. R. Searle's of the naturalist, speech-act, and assertion fallacy's origin in an inadequate understanding of meaning as use, *Speech Acts: An Essay in the Philosophy of Language* (Cambridge, 1969), pp. 131-156.

within the analytic tradition, the restaurative rehabilitation of authority by Gadamer, and the emancipatory interest within the Frankfurt School), they agree on the linguistic and social character of meaning.[21]

This understanding of the relation between language and meaning is significant for language about God. Such theological discourse is not primarily meaningful because it refers to an observable object or experience or to an individual's private "religious" experience.[22] To affirm that it does is to share the same positivistic presuppositions of the critics of the validity of language about. It would then make one's theological discourse vulnerable to the criticism that it is meaningless because it is incapable of verification or merely emotive. Instead, we are suggesting that our language about God is meaningful in its social function[23] and performative nature, whereas the latter should not be privatized as is sometimes done.

I would suggest that religious language functions as meaningful within society because it involves a formulation of an understanding or conviction of a general order of existence and life. It does so by offering an interpretation of both the affirmative and negative within life, of both the joy and the pain of life.[24] Religious language, consequently, constitutes both a discernment of the meaning of joy and pain and a commitment to a way of life consistent with the discernment and consequent to the conviction.

The anomalous experiences of suffering and evil present the most decisive challenge to the religious belief and language about God, especially as creator or source of reality. Religious language necessarily involves a coming to terms with both problems. The problem of suffering could be described as the meaningfulness of suffering, how to suffer, how to make of physical

[21] J. Habermas, *Zur Logik der Sozialwissenschaften* (Frankfurt, 1970); K. Lorenz, *Elemente der Sprachkritik* (Frankfurt, 1970).
[22] See the critical remarks of religious experience as something independent of interpretation by J. Dewey, *A Common Faith* (New Haven, 1943).
[23] Cf. Shailer Mathews, *The Growth of the Idea of God* (New York, 1931).
[24] C. Geertz, "Religion as a Cultural System," in M. Banton (ed.), *Anthropological Approaches to the Study of Religion,* III (London, 1965), pp. 1–46.

pain and personal agony something bearable or sufferable. The problem of suffering easily becomes a problem of evil and involves the reconciliation of the irrationality and inequality of suffering with ethical criteria and normative guides for meaningful order and for human action. Religious discourse must come to terms with the human experience of the ambiguity of suffering and the paradox of evil.

While the religious discourse about this problem in the Old and New Testaments is varied, the language about the joy and pain of God can serve as paradigmatic. Kitamori notwithstanding, pain is never directly predicated of God but only joy is. Deutero-Isaiah (65. 19) is a paradigmatic example of the predication of joy to God. "I will rejoice in Jerusalem and be glad in my people; no more shall be heard in it the sound of weeping and the cry of distress." Here as in Psalms 96 and 97 joy is predicated of God and it has eschatological significance. The suffering and distress of the earth is not explained away, is not given a positive interpretation, is not made a part of the eschatological future. The former troubles are even forgotten (Isa. 65. 16) and man shall share in the joy of God. The same future eschatological orientation is present even in John's Gospel where despite its massive realized eschatology, it is affirmed that sorrow is the lot of the present, but joy is the future eschatological hope (16. 22).

The significance of these paradigmatic statements lies in its acknowledgment of pain as constituting the present alienated lot of man. In so far as pain is not predicated of God the negativity of pain is asserted in so far as it is not eternalized. In so far as not only evil, but also pain and suffering are not predicated of God, they are not made intelligible by being conceptualized as of the essence of the source and goal of the universe, but are only acknowledged as that which we remember in our present state. In short, the meaning of suffering, if not also of evil, does not take place by a reconciliation of facticity with conceptuality, but only through a qualitatively different facticity, which can only be achieved by praxis.

In conclusion, our language about the joy and pain of God is paradigmatic for our language about God because it indicates the extent to which this language functions in a social and performative sense. Our rejection of Kitamori's development of a theology of pain and Moltmann's inter-trinitarian understanding of the pain of God does not mean that we disagree with their plea for a biblical and living pathetic God over against any apathetic and immobile deity. But it does mean that in so far as our language about God signifies a stance or conviction about reality and a commitment to that stance that we refuse to offer a conceptual solution to the problem of suffering and evil, but only acknowledge it as an ambiguity, a surd, and a paradox of the present situation of man. In this perspective, perhaps Karl Rahner's formulation (which Moltmann's strongly criticizes) is more appropriate. His claim that maybe God who cannot suffer in himself can in another is an assertation of the radical facticity of suffering in its otherness and non-identity. In this perspective, the suggestion of Johann B. Metz for a narrative rather than argumentative christology is helpful because it emphasizes that suffering cannot be dialectically mediated by a conceptualized and logically constructed mediation, but only through the memorial and performative character of narratives.[25]

In this discussion of the joy and pain of God, one cannot help but refer to Thomas Aquinas' analysis of our language about God and of the meaning of our theological statement about him. Theological language has both affirmative and negative character. But whereas one can explain in what sense a word is denied of God, one cannot explain in what sense a word is affirmed of God. Consequently theological statements involve not only a negative theology but even as affirmative theological statements they are to be transcended and signify more how God is not than how he is.[26] These reservations about our language about God should lead us to speculate less upon suffering as an inter-trinitarian event, but to concentrate in observing how our language about God has historically functioned and how it can serve the critical, convictional and performative function it can and should have.

[25] J. B. Metz, "Erlösung und Emanzipation," *Stimmen der Zeit* 98 (1973), 171–185, "A Short Apology of Narrative," in *The Crisis of Religious Language,* ed. J. Metz and J. Jossua (New York, 1973).
[26] V. Preller, *Divine Science and the Science of God. A Reformulation of Thomas Aquinas* (New Jersey, 1967).

Gérard Bessière

Humour—A Theological Attitude?

HUMOUR has never allowed itself to be confined within a definition. It has always treated itself with "humour". How shall we approach it? The origins and semantic infancy of the word can be examined, and also the mechanisms that it sets in motion. In the first two somewhat austere sections of this article we shall draw extensively on the little book by that virtuoso of humour, Robert Escarpit.[1] In the third section we shall try to tackle with a smile the immense subject opened up by our title.

I. The Humorous Adventures of a Word

The human phenomenon described in contemporary French by the word "humour" is a universal phenomenon. But it is difficult to talk about it across frontiers, for the forms this phenomenon takes are as varied as the languages, the literary histories and the cultures of the different countries. The reality may seem universal on a vast palette of different shades of colour, but the "word" certainly isn't. It is "humour" in England, but elsewhere it has other names. Moreover, in England ever since the nineteenth century the word has gone hand in hand with a thought-out and relatively coherent tradition which has become a reference point for those trying to analyse and situate "humour".

Its origins are medical—Hippocrates of Cos discerned four "humours" in the human body, related to the four elements.

---

[1] Robert Escarpit, *L'humour* (Paris, 1960).

In the second century, Galen discovered that the cause of sickness lay in an excess of any one of the four "humours". The controversy in England and the whole of Europe in the sixteenth century made "humour" a fashionable word.[2] It was at that time that the English playwright Ben Jonson made use of the term to describe the "character types" in his plays: the choleric type, the melancholy type, the sanguine type and the phlegmatic type. But why did this decisive encounter between "medical quarrels and literary research" not occur elsewhere than in England? According to Escarpit, "there did indeed exist between 1550 and 1650 a sort of European attempt at humour",[3] but its various manifestations were never properly formulated.

Thus "humour" was confined to its island across the Channel for another hundred and fifty years.[4] It came to be seen as a trait peculiar to the English temperament. "The fact of civilization drove out the literary fact without excluding it entirely, but at the end of this development (that is to say in the first quarter of the eighteenth century) humour had achieved the position of being felt as a sort of national trait, as a tradition deriving from the depths of the English soul".[5]

So from the biological predominance of a "humour", through its utilization in the theatre so as to "type" a character, humour ended up by characterizing the psychology of a people.

But if "medical" humour made the transition to "comic" humour, this was because Ben Jonson put his characters in situations "out of plumb"[6] with the humour attributed to them, or he made them display "affected" humours. This duality was favourable to comedy and disclosed at the interior of man, and particularly of "the English soul", "a dialectic between contradictory tendencies of which each served alternately to mask the other.... The whole history of English literature, and of the English soul therein revealed, shows us the double and enigmatic face of a mournful optimism and a cheerful pessimism."[7]

English sense of humour is "the natural and intuitive, but also the lucid and deliberately-smiling awareness of one's own

[2] R. Escarpit, *op. cit.*, pp. 12–13.   [3] R. Escarpit, *op. cit.*, p. 17.
[4] R. Escarpit, *op. cit.*, p. 19.   [5] R. Escarpit, *op. cit.*, p. 20.
[6] R. Escarpit, *op. cit.*, p. 22.   [7] R. Escarpit, *op. cit.*, p. 23.

character and personality in the midst of other persons".[8] It seems to be "the basic condition of that compromise on which the whole of English national life rests. It is equivocation *par excellence,* the no-man's-land of values where—like eccentricity with moral equilibruim—conformism plays hide-and-seek with revolt, smiling with bitterness, and seriousness with scepticism. It is thus that the word proposed by Ben Jonson for the heroes of his plays came to indicate for flesh-and-blood Englishmen a social attitude, a national reflex that Stephen Potter defines thus:

> The general idea is that a common ground has been discovered, perhaps even a safe-conduct giving permission to penetrate the territory of the adversary. But, whether we're ruminating over the humour of others or whether we're creating our own, our most common reflex is detachment through a smile. It is what could be called the English Reflex. It forms part of the fibre of our social life.[9]

The word "humour" continued on its way: it was to abandon the extravagance of the sixteenth century and call for the cool head and serious aspect of the man who "makes others laugh". Escarpit notes the evolution of the word towards objectivity. "For Ben Jonson, one *is* a humour. For Addison, one *has* a humour. For Home one *makes* humour."[10]

Humour became willed. Was it spontaneous or calculated? After 1760, the second alternative gained ground in common usage. In 1771, the *Encyclopaedia Britannica* offered an arbitrary choice between tracking down the thing or tracking down the word: "humour" or "wit".

In *The Spectator* of 10 April 1711 (No. 35), Addison drew up a revealing genealogy. He said that Truth was the founder of the family and begot Common Sense. Common Sense begot Wit who married a lady of a collateral branch, called Gaiety, by whom he had a son: Humour. Humour was thus the youngest of the illustrious family, and as he descended from parents with different dispositions he had a fluctuating and many-sided tem-

[8] R. Escarpit, *op. cit.,* p. 26.
[9] R. Escarpit, *op. cit.,* pp. 26–7. The Stephen Potter message is summarized from *Sense of Humour* (London, 1954), p. 4.
[10] R. Escarpit, *op. cit.,* p. 35.

perament. Sometimes he took on a grave air and a solemn appearance; sometimes he was free and easy and dressed extravagantly, with the result that sometimes he seemed as solemn as a judge and sometimes a joker and a clown. But he derived a great deal from his mother, and whatever his state of soul, he never failed to make people laugh.[11]

"Perhaps it's just a whirligig," remarks Escarpit, "but it is not proved that a whirligig may not be the best way of resolving the problem of humour."[12]

For Thackeray, in the following century, Humour was the son of Wit and Love. Escarpit sees the distinction as slender, for Addison's "gaiety" "is sentimental rather than coldly rational," whereas Wit is "purely intellectual".[13]

In the eighteenth century, humour "split into two. The visible, visceral part—the sense of humour—broke off from the intellectual, conscious, aesthetic part, the part that henceforth the whole world called humour."[14]

It sometimes seems difficult to differentiate humour from wit. But we must never forget humour's mother, "Gaiety". Escarpit recalls Congreve's remark: "Not all men of wit are humorists, but all humorists are men of wit."[15]

It is impossible to pursue the history of the word within the limits of a short article such as this. In France, the word was used by Voltaire in 1725 and was admitted by the *Académie Française* in 1932. The progressive building-up of an international community through our rapid means of communication has contributed over the past decades to the formation of a shared awareness that gives fresh scope to humour.[16] It seems to me, however, that the genealogy of humour quoted above brings to light all the traits it will have at its disposal in its changing, original and historical adventure which is by no means finished.

II. HUMOUR—DIALETICAL HIDE-AND-SEEK

Is the universal phenomenon described by the word "humour" first and foremost affective or intellectual? If affective, then it

[11] Quoted by R. Escarpit, *op. cit.*, p. 38.   [12] *Ibid*.
[13] R. Escarpit, *op. cit.*, p. 39.   [14] R. Escarpit, *op. cit.*, p. 40.
[15] Quoted by R. Escarpit, *op. cit.*, p. 41.
[16] R. Escarpit, *op. cit.*, p. 63-4.

involves the humorist's whole personality and plays its part in ⌐
his relations with other people. If essentially intellectual, then
it does not involve its author but is akin to the comic or dramatic
action and technique which makes use of displacement "by
transposing the natural expression of an idea into another key."[17]⌐

This transposition comes about through a suspension of judgment, whether this be affective judgment, moral judgment,
philosophical judgment or judgment of the comic—to quote
the categories used by L. Cazamian in his analysis.[18] But Escarpit
points out that the transposition mechanism here described is
not enough to produce humour. Humour requires involvement
of the humorist's intentions and also the state of mind of those to
whom he is addressing himself: "One of the constants of humour
is benevolence of intention, or at least a spirit of toleration."[19]
Escarpit quotes the anglicist, Floris Delattre: "It transforms
laughter into a broad but tolerant benevolence, not too far indeed
from charity."[20]

Jean Château permits an alliance between the "intellectualist"
and "affectivist" points of view. "Everything leads us to suppose
that we are confronted with two worlds ... a serious world,
the ordinary world of our work, of our everyday life, and a non-
serious world, divided into compartments, in contradiction to
the first."[21] "The non-serious world brings an essentially human
capacity into play, that of differentiating between the levels of
the universe and of sliding from one to the other."[22] But, to this
"intellectualist" datum, he adds: "The non-serious world may
be mutual love, communication. The joke is a social good; it
carries on the smile, which is the doorstep to the human. To
smile is sometimes to show that one is not so serious as might
appear, it is to palliate censure, to ensure a spiritual communion

[17] H. Bergson, *Le rire* (Paris, 1950), p. 93.
[18] L. Cazamian, "Pourquoi nous ne pouons pas définir l'humour,"
Revue Germanique (1906), p. 610. Quoted by R. Escarpit, *op. cit.*, p. 5,
note 2.
[19] R. Escarpit, *op. cit.*, p. 82.
[20] Floris Delattre, "La naissance de l'humour dans la vielle Angleterre",
Revue anglo-américaine (1927), p. 307. Quoted by R. Escarpit, *op. cit.*,
p. 82.
[21] J. Château, "Le sérieux et ses contraires", *Revue philosophique*
(October-December, 1950), p. 449. Quoted by R. Escarpit, *op. cit.*, p. 84.
[22] *Ibid.*, p. 456. Quoted by R. Escarpit, *op. cit.*, p. 82.

that the over-serious man knows nothing of. To smile is sometimes to deflect the other from the closed world of self-interest
so as to lure him into communion with the non-serious. All the
more reason why laughter should consolidate the union of
laughers; laughter has a social role (if not a social source, as
Bergson wrongly thought) like humour—that blend of the
serious and the non-serious."[23]

Escarpit points out that there is laughter without humour
and humour without laughter, and he invites us to recognize
that "what is called laughter, like what is called humour, contains phenomena of dialectical structure, comprising a critical
phase generative of anguish and nervous tension, and a constructive phase of relaxation, conquest and balance. As humour
is especially concerned with the higher (that is to say conscious)
regions of laughter, its critical phase is intellectual and we shall
call it irony. Its constructive phase is almost (but not absolutely)
always affective, and for want of a better term we shall define
it as the 'rebound' of humour."[24]

This "rebound" comes about through a sort of complicity
with the humorist and his capacities of reconstruction which are
very closely allied to the social group.

Escarpit sees this "rebound" of humour as bringing about four
"conquests": the "conquest" of security, of sympathy, of involvement and of transcendence.[25]

The conquest of security exploits the "tension-relaxation"
mechanism and the frequent intervention of a feeling of superior-
ity: those who laugh at the story about the lunatic look on
themselves as being totally sane. The conquest of sympathy
brings into play in humour the intervention of the "collusive
wink" which "rectifies destructive irony"; this collusion also
creates security, through the sharing of the same condition. The
conquest of involvement allows humour to be "a weapon of
war".[26] By making fun of the enemy or of the situation, it gets
rid of anguish and brings solidarities into play. Caricatures of
politicians and satirical newspapers exploit the possibilities of
this involvement. In showing what he means by the conquest

[23] *Ibid.*, p. 457. Quoted by R. Escarpit, *op. cit.*, p. 85.
[24] R. Escarpit, *op. cit.*, p. 86.   [25] R. Escarpit, *op. cit.*, pp. 111–25.
[26] R. Escarpit, *op. cit.*, p. 117.

of transcendence, Escarpit quotes Joseph Moreau's reflections on the mechanism of Socratic irony, which comprises a "need for conversion". "If Socratic irony is opposed to received values, and if it therefore sometimes has revolutionary overtones, this is not so as to destroy values, but so as to test them, reform them, build them. But values of opinion can only be built up through an appeal to the values of interiority, which are produced by thought, and which reveal to man his transcendent origin, his eternal destiny. Socratic irony opens the way to a religious conception of man and that is what justifies it and saves it ... without this demand for conversion and this opening-up to the divine, irony would be no more than a highly questionable mental eccentricity. Only the mystic has the right to be ironical—you have to believe in something, have faith in something that goes beyond man, if you want to engage in ironical banter about the conduct and opinions of the common man."[27]

Escarpit ends up by seeing in humour "an art of living". "It's a whim and at the same time a means of breaking the fatally maternal automatisms that life in society, and just life by itself, create around us as a protection and a winding-sheet.... Humour bursts open the cocoon in the direction of life, of progress, of risk. Usually the only thing that emerges is a base and uninteresting mite, but now and again the bright-coloured butterfly of laughter springs out, like that of the gods, or else one discerns in the darkness the mysterious unfolding of the wings of some nocturnal moth."[28]

III. THE LAUGHTER OF THE ANGELS

In his book, *A Rumour of Angels*, Peter Berger echoes Freud's and Bergson's theories that the comic is linked to the perception of a discordance, a disproportion. But according to Berger there is a basic discordance from which all the other discordances capable of producing laughter flow—namely, the discordance

[27] J. Moreau, in the course of a debate on humour. See *Bulletin du Centre d'Études de Littérature Générale*, Faculté des lettres, Bordeaux, VII (1957–58–59), meeting of 21 January 1958. Quoted by R. Escarpit, *op. cit.*, p. 121.
[28] R. Escarpit, *op. cit.*, p. 127.

between man and the universe. By dealing with the imprisonment of the human spirit (in the world) by laughter, humour
manages to imply that the imprisonment is not definitive, that
one day it will be overcome. Thus humour also becomes an
index of transcendence—and in this case takes the form of a
discreet call to redemption.[29] This being so, "the actions of a
clown take on a sacramental dignity" (sic!).

Is it permitted to search for this "index of transcendence"
with the smile, taking Freud as our guide? Freud quotes the
remark of a criminal who was taken to the gallows on a Monday
and cried out: "The week's starting well!" And he comments:
"The essence of humour resides in the fact that one spares oneself the emotions to which the situation should rightly lead and
puts oneself beyond such affective demonstrations by means of
a joke."[30]

Humour is thus a method "by which we withdraw from the
constraint of suffering" and by which Freud questions his saga-
city as psychoanalyst. "Is it then reasonable to say that one
treats oneself as though one was a child and at the same time
plays the superior role of an adult towards that child?" We are
reminded of Kierkegaard's assertion, though we lack the space
to examine it with the attention it deserves: "The cultivation of
the spirit with respect to the absolute, put side by side with the
childish soul, produces humour."[31]

Humour would therefore derive from parental influence
seeming to say: "Look! There's the world that seems so dangerous to you! A child's game! So the best thing is to joke!"[32]
Thus humour would be a breath of childhood—at a time when
many are worrying about the grim necessities of reality. And
the question of the "index" can follow: Is this childhood illu-
sory, is it an absurd attempt to get back to the mother's womb?
Or might it perhaps be the strange and fantastic evidence of
another reality, another childhood, another parental influence
that would get level with the future?

[29] P. Berger, *A Rumour of Angels, Modern Society and the Rediscovery of the Supernatural*. (New York, 1969.)
[30] S. Freud, "L'humour", article in *Image* (1928), XIV, part 1.
[31] S. Kierkegaard, *Post scriptum* (Paris, 1949), p. 372.
[32] S. Freud, *art. cit.*

humor = the sign of presence of god !

At this point we must make a crucial and logical pause. Have you noticed that humour and love get along very well together? This connivance must conceal some secret. Humour blossoms readily in those who love and know themselves to be loved. Like something that eases life.

If I may risk a solemn affirmation, I would say that there is no love without humour. For love without humour underestimates the distance, and hence also the respect, and the infinite quest for encounter, between two beings. Love without humour knows nothing of the surprise that is "the other", it makes every effort to pull him back to itself, it narrows the world. It no longer believes in the "unbelievable". It is nothing but possession, and hence solitude. But true love, like humour, knows that there are a number of worlds, a number of characters, a number of people, dialectics and complicity always coming to fresh life in the encounter.

The high path at the crest of love is a perpetual birth. It creates and recreates the beings who give themselves to it. It brings all the roles into play. Those who love are spouses to each other, father and mother, children. From childish expressions of tenderness to the silences of pure presence ... what does this gamut of loving attitudes signify? Whence comes this ever-new being which unites those who love? It seems to spring from themselves while going beyond them, like a child coming from elsewhere. . . . Here too we have the son of Wit and Gaiety, impervious to the conditionings of life, and brimming over with benevolence.

All right, I'm showing my hand, and so much the worse or so much the better if people laugh at me: humour is the sign of the presence of God in mankind. But not of any old God and not of any old presence. If humour is the "index of transcendence" it turns round immediately on the person who claims to unmask it. The clown "whose actions take on a sacramental dignity" (!!) bursts out laughing in front of the theologian. If "religion gives the comic all its significance and justifies laughter",[33] then humour in its turn can bathe even theology in its dancing light. To the theological significance of humour,

---

[33] P. Berger, *op. cit.,* p. 114.

it will immediately respond with a humorous treatment of theology.

Escarpit makes a wholesome diagnostic of it. All domains of social existence are successively overtaken by humour which brings them relaxation, freedom of spirit, the capacity to take over destiny. "In our world which is stretched almost to breaking point, there is nothing that can survive too much seriousness." But he adds: "Religion still seems unscathed. Let us hope for the sake of those who believe in it that it will not remain so for long, or it will perish."[34] Well, well!

So, this warning having been given, let us say: the man without humour, even if he's the pope, doesn't know God. He sees in the mirror of his seriousness nothing but the image of his essential fears or the projection of collective necessities. Popular wisdom has always known it: "A sad saint is a sorry saint." And Barth was able to write: "Theology is a joyful science."[35]

No love without humour, and reciprocally. And no life with God without humour. God cannot creep into manhood and escape the "small and hampered"[36] eternity to which we want to relegate him except through some immaterial breaches: love and humour. We gain experience in those moments when we are larger—and smaller—than ourselves. When we are between "us" and "ourselves". The sense of humour enjoys these limping and ambiguous expressions.

Humour reveals to the husband that he is only "half" himself, because of his wife, and that the "life of his life" rests in a woman, born of a "rib" taken from him while he was asleep! Humour teaches man that no conditioning altogether conditions him, and that everything that offers him resistance can also support him, as water supports fish. A word, a smile, are enough to make him feel that he is other than what he undergoes, creates or savours. The man who reacts with humour to the event that crushes him reveals the measureless measure of man. The man who smiles in face of his death already lives his immortality. Humour is a quiver of transcendence within the weight of mankind. "A higher revolt of the spirit", as Auguste

[34] R. Escarpit, op. cit., p. 72.
[35] In "Pour une théologie évangélique" (French trans.) (Geneva), p. 115.
[36] The image comes from G. K. Chesterton's Orthodoxy.

Breton said? Reactivation of "parental influence"? Yes, if you like, as if man were indefinitely his own child whom he watches at play, in a groping initiation to another, disproportionate future.... As if man were also, and oddly, the child of Another who is hiding.

The freshest type of humour—the humour of certain saints—knows that the path we tread unfolds in front of the unique and inexpressible Father, the Father from whom all fatherhood, all love and all laughter come. It is he, with an originality that belongs to him alone, who is the "parental influence" (and more than parental!) over the childhoods to come. He, in going towards whom we become children, in laughable contradiction to the best-established spatio-temporal evidence! For—to quote some lines from Gilles Deleuze, whose writings far outstrip my intellectual capacities—"what is deeper than any depth is the surface, the skin.... Humour is the art of surfaces and top layers, of roving eccentricities and of the contingent point that is always out of place, it is the art of static genesis, the *savoir-faire* of the pure happening, or the 'fourth person singular'—all significance, designation and manifestation suspended, all height and depth abolished."[37] And so on and so on and so on, I feel like summarizing! No words, mouth agape, the leaping of life's pulsation towards.... Or: emptiness accepted in the sense that one doesn't "possess", availability from the field to the heaven that goes beyond it and acts upon it, the horizon made by the landscape through espousing the immaterial line of light.

Humour readily changes its area of activity and jumps into the disproportion between man and reality; it sets in motion interior freedom, it has a sense of the relative, it unknots absolutes which are not absolutes except from a predetermined point of view. No man's word can escape its airy harassment.

And how about theology? We shall begin with a time-honoured axiom: *Quidquid accipitur, ad modum recipientis recipitur,* and we shall continue with a Chinese proverb: "When someone points to the moon, the idiot looks at his finger." Theology, hitherto chaperoned by Dame Orthodoxy whom no

[37] G. Deleuze, *Logique du sens,* 10/18 (Paris, 1960), p. 190.

one has ever seen to smile,[38] has kept company with the Serious much more than she has flirted with Humour. She has just tolerated the somersaults of this turbulent boy on the slopes of Apologetics, of Exhortation and of Preaching, by directing his dynamism towards "others". What would happen if the queen summoned the king's jester in these times of gloomy sterility?

The immediate removal of all idols would be the first necessity, including those that camouflage intellectual or institutional misrepresentations. Then people would get frightened: "You're pulling everything down ... what's going to be left?"—but from time to time the exchange of a smile or an infectious burst of laughter would show that the path was leading somewhere. We would pass near Jonah's castor-oil plant, and from behind the aged Sarah's tent we would hear her laugh: we are born of that laugh and of a sterile woman! We would listen for a moment to the light breeze on Mount Horeb; while suspending theological judgment we would perceive the disproportions, we would go from one point of view to the other, like children playing a game of theological "feet-off-ground" catch. Humorous theology could play with affirmative theology and negative theology, and would be very much at home with the old narrative theology. It would contribute to making those old stories re-echo within us—those open-ended stories that our lives endlessly repeat and prolong. We would see the grain of mustard seed flying in the wind of the Spirit, and our smile would become "the doorstep to the human" and to the divine. We could even go as far as "the theology of the absurd" which some people practise without realizing it, and as far as "theology-fiction" so as to forecast other moves and other futures.

And always with that collusive, benevolent, creative wink which draws men together and tells them that after the void of the leap their feet will find solid ground again so that they can continue on their way. "He that has ears to hear, let him hear."

For on this road to Emmaus we would soon be joined by an ardent-faced man who is always ready to let a unique form of

---

[38] Bultmann wrote: "Orthodoxy has no humour." *Glauben und Verstehen,* II, p. 269.

Jesus

humour spring from his silences. "The Kingdom of God"—
do you realize? THE KINGDOM OF GOD—is like a woman
sweeping, is like a grain of mustard seed, is like a dishonest
steward! The circle of listeners is there, waiting for the moment
when they will understand and burst out laughing.
How can anyone say that Jesus never laughed? How can
anyone present him as a solemn man, a long-faced type? When
all the time he was telling stories at meals that brought him into
contact with all sorts of people; when he was handling the
parable with a lightness of touch that theological exegesis and
argumentation have often totally ignored! Who will convey
the humour of Jesus? "From the stones of the road I can raise
up sons of Abraham! ... Destroy this Temple and in three
days I shall build it again! ... The Kingdom of God is like a
handful of leaven...." What a distance between these words,
weighed down with expectation, with desire, with the past, and
the way in which Jesus swells them with the future!
Jesus was at home with all the refinements of oriental humour,
and how often his adversaries bore the cost of it. "Simon, I'm
going to ask you a question..." The Samaritan woman was not
without humour either, but as he had more of it than she, she
suddenly became serious. He asked for new goat-skin bottles
when everyone knew that wine spoiled except in old ones. And
if the situation became awkward, he said to his companions:
"Consider the birds of the air...."
Jesus didn't much care for exemplary attitudes that produced
boredom: he speaks of pearl-merchants and their audacity. "Let
the man who is without sin throw the first stone," he said to
those who accused the woman taken in adultery, and they all
went away, beginning with the oldest!
Jesus made use of irony and even insolence, both with sover-
eign freedom and humour. His humour was always opening
doors, he broke down all human enclosures, whether that of
man's heart, that of the society of his time, that of Judaism and
the synagogue. What would he say today about the ossification
of our nations, of our churches, of our theologies? What ex-
plosive questions would he put? What parables would he give
us to smile at so as to overcome our solemnities?

IV. Envoi

For some time now it has been the done thing, at least in France, to say that "God has a sense of humour." A facile formula, perhaps, but wouldn't it be a way of exorcizing an unavowed anguish and of escaping from the gravity of contemporary problems?

That troubadour of humorous theology, Chesterton, trod these paths with more subtlety. In *The Man who was Thursday*, Mr Sunday was both the cheerful chief of the terrorists and the mysterious chief of police. "You will understand the sea, and I shall be still a riddle; you shall know what the stars are, and not know what I am. Since the beginning of the world all men have hunted me like a wolf—kings and sages, and poets and law-givers, all the churches, and all the philosophies. But I have never been caught yet, and the skies will fall in the time I turn to bay."[39]

We are dealing with God, who goes on from the heart of his mystery: "I sent you out to war. I sat in the darkness, where there is not any created thing, and to you I was only a voice commanding valour and unnatural virtue. You heard the voice in the dark, and you never heard it again. The sun in heaven denied it, the earth and sky denied it, all human wisdom denied it. And when I met you in the daylight I denied it myself.... But you were men. You did not forget your secret honour, though the whole cosmos turned an engine of torture to tear it out of you."[40]

Finally Sunday's face grew to the measure of the universe, and over it there spread the suffering smile of Christ. When the vision had disappeared one of the characters, the poet-policeman, felt himself deeply transformed.

"But Syme could only feel an unnatural buoyancy in his body and a crystal simplicity in his mind that seemed to be superior to everything that he said or did. He felt he was in possession of some impossible good news, which made every other thing a triviality, but an adorable triviality."[41]

[39] G. K. Chesterton, *The Man who was Thursday* (London, 1937), pp. 154–5. Quoted by R. Escarpit, *op. cit.*, p. 122.
[40] *Ibid.*, R. Escarpit, pp. 122–3.
[41] *Ibid.*

Conversion towards which the dialectics of humour lead!
It was fear that created the gods, said the ancient thinker.
But those gods are dead, or anyway dying. How if it were
humour that created—and welcomed—the God of the future?
By always smiling at the ephemeral garments with which the
religions clothe man's nudity before "Him". If there were an
urgent and ceaseless conversion to humour on the part of all
theology. . . .

Translated by Barbara Wall

Jacques Colette

Joy, Pleasure and Anguish: Thoughts on Barth and Mozart

"THE flesh is sad, alas," says the Poet. And so is truth, say the last of the romantics. "Love, love ..." is the cry of preachers —and songs. But Eros and Thanatos go hand in hand, comments Freud. Karl Barth, whose splendid theology is made up of passion and objectivity,[1] sees in Mozart's music the triumphal expression of ultimate joy. His celebration of Mozart is a symptom worthy of our attention, something much more than a fleeting digression in the system or a dose of humour intended to temper the solemnity of dogmatic construction.

Whether the allusions to Mozart occur in his *Church Dogmatics* or in his occasional writings, they certainly have their place and significance in the Barthian system. Although their place is fairly easy to locate, their significance is rather more difficult to analyse. An examination of this double question at once draws together the theologian and the philosopher. Like any other philosopher, Barth had to find a place for artistic creation within his coherent discourse—artistic creation, that cry of mankind confronted with destiny. If we refuse to let ourselves be won over purely and simply by the enthusiasm of "Barth, the lover of Mozart",[2] the question arises of deciding under what heading to situate his brief but important digressions on art. And this question gives rise to another: what is the meaning of all his comments about the joy and sadness, the

[1] H. Urs von Balthasar, *Karl Barth. Darstellung und Deutung seiner Theologie* (Cologne, 1951), p. 36.
[2] *Ibid.*

96

childlike spirit, play and the function of art in society and in
the context of religion? What—in the eyes of the theologian—
is the significance of masterpieces, those brilliant anticipations
that carry man beyond anguish, boredom, work and pain?

I. BARTH AND MOZART

Karl Barth had listened to Mozart in his childhood and, from
then onwards "Mozart and none other"[3] became part of his
existence. For Barth, "the childlike intuition ... of what is at
once the beginning and end of all things" shone through Mozart's music, music "that delights, refreshes, consoles," that
transports us "to the threshold of a good and ordered world."
It was impossible not to conclude that there existed "a direct
and very special relationship between God and this man".[4] The
infant prodigy, according to Barth, was also an infant-adult, he
knew the whole of reality, "joy and pain, good and evil, life
and death in their reality, hence also in their limitations".[5] Total
knowledge that always leads "from darkness towards light, and
never conversely",[6] knowledge that embraces the movement of
"things as they are".[7] Though announcing no message, Mozart
liberates his hearer and, without claiming to do so, proclaims
"the praise of God",[8] for he sees that everything comes from
God and everything goes to God.

It is hardly surprising that such an inspired view of life should
have been united to an awareness of angels. Barth referred to
angelology and eschatology in a lecture given in Basle on 29
January 1945.[9] Angels are always at play, he said, they know
nothing of tragedy and therefore Mozart, as "a man without
problems, truly free in his innermost heart,[10] belonged to them.
What a misconception to evoke the demoniacal in his regard,
as did Kierkegaard![11] Peace was already granted to this man

---

[3] For this and the following quotations, see the text in the *Luzerner
Neueste Nachrichten* (21 January 1956), translated into French in K.
Barth, *Wolfgang Amadeus Mozart, 1756–1956.* (Geneva, ²1969), pp. 5–12.
[4] *Ibid.*, p. 14.   [5] *Ibid.*, p. 21.   [6] *Ibid.*, p. 22.
[7] *Ibid.*, p. 22.   [8] *Ibid.*, p. 27.   [9] *Ibid.*, pp. 31 ff.
[10] *Ibid.*, p. 42.
[11] See *ibid.*, pp. 41–3. Don Juan himself is qualified as "hero", no less.
(*Ibid.*, p. 44).

who had heard the echoes of victory over evil. The contemporary of *eschaton* could create music which was a parable of the Kingdom of Heaven where angels revolve within the twofold splendour of worship and harmony.[12] His music is concrete because it knows nothing of the abstraction of evil and vibrates with the "yes" and the "amen" to creation. It is "total"[13] because it celebrates the positive aspect of creation, the aspect that prevails definitively over the negative.

II. EVIL, MUSIC AND THE PHILOSOPHIES

The thesis is plain: "Mozart belongs to theology".[14] With regard to the good creation in its totality, Mozart knew something "that the true Fathers of the Church, including our Reformers ... did not know or were at any rate unable to express".[15] In face of the problem of evil and nothingness, Mozart's work prepared the way far better than "any scientific argument".[16] Although he accorded this privilege to the artist, the seer, Barth the theologian none the less confronted scientifically the philosophical tradition concerning the themes of evil and sadness, optimism and pessimism. With regard to nothingness—whether by this we understand the dark side of creation or the reality that is opposed to the Creator himself—the Barthian attitude, faced with the optimism of Leibniz and the eighteenth century in general, is many-sided. The optimism in question could be a thesis very near to Christian optimism, and yet this nearness should not disguise the differences. The optimism of the men of the Enlightenment in fact underestimated the virulence and imminence of the threat brought to mankind by death, sin and the devil. Moreover the imperialistic anthropocentrism of this rationalism turned God into a mere reflection of the perfection discovered in man and the universe, and consequently underestimated the free decision of the Creator and the Saviour in relation to the world and sinful man. In spite of this, we can speak of an "at any rate formal affinity with the teaching of

[12] Their music of adoration also gives a voice to the silent world. See *Church Dogmatics*, III, 3, 2, § 51, 2.
[13] *Church Dogmatics*, *ibid.*, § 50, 2.
[14] *Ibid.*, p. 10.   [15] *Ibid.*   [16] *Ibid.*, p. 11.

the gospel. It is not by chance that the eighteenth century produced the best music of all time—J. S. Bach, Handel, Gluck
and Haydn and the incomparable Mozart".[17] After the great
depression of the nineteenth century, the Christian was not sure
"whether a Leibniz himself, that is to say whether absolute
optimism presented under another guise, might not one day
come back. Besides who can say whether it wouldn't be splendid,
from one point of view at least, to live again in a Leibnizian
century?"[18]

The understanding of Christianity "purely and simply as a
triumphal cause" implies the "refutation of the basic Kierkegaardian thesis regarding the separation between aesthetics and
religious ethics". Here again the interpretation of Mozart is the
criterion—where Kierkegaard hears demoniacal accents, Barth
hears angelic voices. In fact, "the religious is aesthetic when it
shows itself to be glory and splendour, because it is here that
it is most authentically itself".[19]

According to Hegel,[20] Christian art was art in which the
spiritual element prevailed, "an effort on the part of art to go
beyond itself".[21] It was in Christian art that "art's loftiest destination" was best exemplified, "the destination it holds in common with religion and philosophy. As with these, it is a way
of expressing the divine ... and it often constitutes the only
way of understanding the religion of a people".[22] Modern man
—as witness of the historical fulfilment of the Christian religion
(the Reformation)—knows that "romantic or Christian art has
realized its maximum from the point of view of the idea." But
he also knows that "the idea only truly exists in the spirit"[23] and
that in consequence "the work of art is incapable of satisfying
our ultimate need for the absolute".[24]

Could Barth be compared to Hegel because, for him too,
"Christian" music—which means the incomparable Mozart—is
a prefiguration of the music of the angels? It prefigures, no less,

[17] *Ibid.*, p. 440.   [18] *Ibid.*, p. 441.
[19] H. Urs von Balthasar, *op. cit.*
[20] In the final analysis the Hegelian system was, for Barth ,"a great
question, a great disillusionment and perhaps, none the less, a great promise"
(*Die protestanische Theologie im 19. Jahrhundert*, end of ch. 10).
[21] *Ibid.*, p. 32. See Hegel, *Introduction to Aesthetics.*
[22] Hegel, *ibid.*   [23] *Ibid.*   [24] *Ibid.*

the eschatological harmony at the heart of which alone shall our need for the absolute be able to blossom in the celebration of religion and the cosmos reconciled in a single act of praise. But we must beware of making this comparison. Hegel was nearer to what is happening today when he observed that, though we are still capable of admiration and delight, we no longer see in art the unsurpassable manifestation of the absolute. "Our attitude with regard to the creations of art is much colder and more rational".[25] This accounts for those countless analyses which examine the *what* and the *how* of the artistic output of various societies and epochs. Stemming from Hegel are those cohorts of researchers who—in ethnology, psycho-sociology and psychoanalysis—try to find within what we call culture "the function of art and its place in the totality of our lives".[26]

III. BARTH AND CONTEMPORARY APPROACHES TO ARTISTIC ACTIVITY

As Geoffrey Clive has remarked, Kierkegaard would have severely rebuked Karl Barth for having related the almighty and holy aspects of God to the typically Mozartian reaction towards the demoniacal ways of providence.[27] Judging by *Don Giovanni*[28] it would seem that the master-theme of the punishment of the dissolute man concerns what P. J. Jouve has called the demoniacal link between Don Juan and the Father.[29] What

[25] *Ibid.*
[26] *Ibid.* Certainly Hegel was not only the "forefather" of the sciences of man—inasmuch as he foresaw their place and their significance when they were proposing to analyse artistic experience and production. He was also the philosopher for whom those studies could not possibly replace the achievements of the Spirit in religion and philosophy. Heidegger pointed out, as a characteristic of our time, "the entry of the work of art into the visual field of aesthetics"; see his *Holzwege* (Frankfurt, 1950), pp. 69–70. In a world without the Absolute, abandoned by the gods, myths and studies of myths proliferate. In a world where art is no longer the voice of the Absolute, aesthetics comes forward as a science with its departments, its institutes, its researchers.
[27] *The Demonic in Mozart* in *"Music and Letters"*, XXXVII, 1 (January 1956), p. 2.
[28] One can say *a fortiori* of *Don Giovanni* what J. Chailley says of *The Magic Flute*, quoting the letter of 8 October 1791: As a musician, Mozart was by no means indifferent to his libretto; see his *Musique et Esotérisme: "La Flûte enchantée" opéra maçonnique* (Paris, 1968), pp. 24–5; 309–10.
[29] See P. J. Jouve, *Le Don Juan de Mozart* (Fribourg, 1942), pp. 247,

could be more demoniacal, in fact, than the startling transition
from life to death, a culmination "more supernatural than religious",[20] than the career, the challenge, the happiness, "the
whirlwind airy with desire" of this "sinner without sin"?[31]

Between the seraphic, mystical Mozart and the libertarian,
revolutionary Mozart, we have to find our way back to the historical reality[32] of this musician who was filled with the ideas
of the Enlightenment and of Viennese freemasonry and who was
also the seemingly naïve author of the most deliberately scato-
logical letters. We cannot be satisfied with seeing here and there
inspired and innocent games of humour and the spirit of childhood. We must drop the idea of the *images d'Epinal*, not without recalling while doing so that the child, according to
Baudelaire and Freud, and according to Hobbes and Diderot
before them, is innocent only through lack of strength.[33]

Mozart confronted death like the martyr revolting against
repose, but he encountered "this true and excellent friend of
man"[34] by dance and play with which is blended the joy of
Hyperion and the anguish of the modern soul faced with
nothingness. Tirelessly but actively subjected to the demands of
sensuality, capable at the same time of lending his voice to the
religious sensibility of his time, Mozart was not one of his own
heroes. Neither a martyr nor a criminal, he sang. He admirably

---

255, 257–8. See also D. Fernandez' study based on psychoanalysis, "La
figure du Père dans les Opéras de Mozart", in *L'Arbre jusqu'aux racines*
(Paris, 1972): "Leopold had been dead for five months at the time of the
first performance of *Don Giovanni*. Those who suppose that this event
'liberated' Mozart have not listened to the opera. One can only liberate
oneself from the father by killing him, and one can only kill him by
exchanging a relative subjection for absolute fascination" (p. 274).

[20] P. J. Jouve, *op. cit.*, p. 266.

[31] *Ibid.*, p. 39.

[32] See the justified severity of L. Rebatet, *Une histoire de la musique*
(Paris, 1969), for the Mozart of Henri Ghéon and François Mauriac as
for the anticlerical, Jacobin, extreme republican Mozart of J. and B.
Massin, *W. A. Mozart* (Paris, 1959).

[33] See J. Starobinski, *L'oeil vivant*, II (Paris, 1970), p. 265, quoting
Hobbes: *Ita ut vir malus idem fere sit quod puer robustus.*

[34] Letter from Mozart to his father, 4 April 1787. On Mozart's initiation
and admission to the heart of freemasonry in the spirit of religious
toleration going beyond the particularity of rites and religions, see the
comment on this letter by J. Chailley, *op. cit.*, pp. 26, 75–6.

proclaimed "the ruptures that life endures at the hand of death",[35] and he could do this because for him it was the only way of not opposing good and evil, life and death, as rival hypostases. It was the only means of evolving in the confused element of their intermingling.

When he initiated the awareness of nihilism, Kierkegaard was well aware that it fell to the artist to celebrate that ambiguity where the comic and the tragic merge, the religious irreligiosity characteristic of our time. Music, especially capable of expressing the instant, sensuality, the leap, repetition, can also lull to sleep and mystify. Art at the service of playful error is essentially subversive. The anguish and instability of the game characterize our epoch. This, according to Kierkegaard, accounts for the infatuation for Mozart, who was the first to translate this sensibility into apparently simple and traditional music.

We know that Kierkegaard remained resolutely critical of all inspired aesthetic interiority, now and henceforth theocentrically orientated and liberating with regard to all oppression through necessity. Infinitely tolerated despair characterizes the aesthetic period. The revelation of a new immediacy is of another order. It would appear unseemly to suspect K. Barth, the theologian of the transcendence of the Word of God, of having made light of that.[36] And yet what he says about Mozart speaks in favour of a reconciliation between the aesthetic and the religious, an idea that would have been very foreign to the Danish thinker. This reconciliation is thinkable and possible only if the religious is conceived as a higher pleasure to which man could give himself as he gives himself aesthetically to passionate and anguished impatience in the moment of enjoyment.

Certainly the demoniacal must be fairly close if an outcome can be found only in a religion that has broken from every form of immanentist humanism, through humour—in the Kierkegaardian sense of the word.

Many recent works have treated art as tracing a descent into

[35] P. J. Jouve, op. cit., p. 267.
[36] We recall the homage paid to Kierkegaard by K. Barth in the preface to the 2nd edition of his Römerbrief (Munich, 1921). "If I have a 'system' at all, it is that I try to keep what Kierkegaard called the 'infinite qualitative distinction' of time and eternity in both its negative and its positive aspects and constantly as possible in mind."

hell. Maurice Blanchot's thought, in particular, is always turning on this "other night" from which Orpheus and the Commander return.[37] Here we are dealing with myth "inasmuch as
the Christian world has not spiritualized it".[38] It is then that we
can see in Don Juan the superb hero, the healthy, brave and
vital man. As for the guest of stone, he has the coldness and
"the frozen hugeness of 'the other night' " : "outwardly colder
and more anonymous than Christian death".[39] Don Juan dining
with the Commander is the challenge addressed to the imper-
sonality and coldness of stone, that is to say to the nocturnal
face of desire.

Just as "the higher enjoyment of humour"[40] breaks away
from the oppressive weight of life, so does art. Art procures
the "reward of seduction", the "preliminary pleasure" that permits us "to enjoy henceforth our own phantasms without shame
or scruple".[41] Here we are touching on the cathartic function of
art that has been recognized since the time of Aristotle. The
work of art is nothing other than the witness to an unfulfilled
desire, that of deciphering the night.[42] The work of art does not
reflect the truth and splendour of Being. Its success is not in
the order of soothing reconciliation, such as is sought by the
various academic forms. Coming from a setting other than the
domain of sounds and words,[43] the figure that presides over the
sonata, the symphony, the opera—the "Poem"—is concerned
with desire and death. The production of a work demands that

[37] See L'espace littéraire (Paris, 1955), pp. 178–84, and the comment on
Hölderlin's Gottes Fehl hilft, ibid., pp. 185 ff.
[38] L'entretient infini (Paris, 1969), p. 281.
[39] Ibid., p. 283.
[40] Freud, Der Dichter und das Phantasieren (1908).
[41] Ibid., p. 81.
[42] See J. F. Lyotard, Dérive à partir de Marx et Freud (Paris, 1973), p. 60.
[43] For the analysis of which, no technique is too rigorous. Barth's
allusions to the musical domain arise from what Alban Berg called "the
musical description" to evoke "the limits beyond which it should not go
under pain of becoming intolerable at this time." In works worthy of the
name, there is never artistic impulse without technical ability, hence "we
have the . . . duty to ask questions in the technical sphere . . . if we want
to be able to make judgments on the subject of music"; see "A. Berg, inter-
prète de Schumann," adapted by J. Brunschwig, in Contrepoints, VII
(1949), pp. 48, 52–3. "The dream of every critic is to be able to define
an art by its technique" (Roland Barthès).

one walks on the edge of an abyss. Not turned in on itself, having renounced the privileges of sovereignty, the *ego* of the artist frees itself for pleasure only at the price of great risks, by giving itself to extreme ordeals. We must remember not only Hölderlin, Goya and Van Gogh, but also Dante and Shakespeare. The myth of the artist—child at play—does not stand up to examination even were the artist called Mozart. As Plato taught, the true catharsis is death. Art is in its image.

All honour to Barth for having recognized that Mozart, more than anyone else, represents a happy moment, but one without illusions, between the eighteenth century and its philosophy of pre-established harmony, and the nineteenth century, which brought such great psychical, aesthetic and historical upheavals.

But the purely verbal humour of his allusions to the "divine Mozart" can give no idea of where this music leads. Under its exclusive form, the worship bestowed on it derives from a literary genre in process of disappearance. Even when totally transfigured in the unreal beauty of the total spectacle, the path to death loses none of its tragedy. As for faith in an ultimate victory, sole resort of a "joy that endures", how could it come to terms with the sublime flashes of a Don Juan, a Faust or a Sarastro?

Translated by Barbara Wall

PART III
CONCRETE EXAMPLES

Ernesto Cardenal

The Gospel in Solentiname

"There was no place for them in the inn"
(Luke 2. 7).

IT IS Christmas, and in the little church of Solentiname we are celebrating Midnight Mass the day after the destruction of Managua. In that town, as I remind them, the wealth and the grimmest poverty in the country existed side by side. I tell them that the Christmas which the city was getting ready to celebrate was not Christ's; it belonged to the god of money. Managua's suffering tonight, and the suffering of the whole country, has more in common with the painful scene described in the gospel of Mary without a house and having to give birth to the Son of God among the animals. Another thing I mention is that some hours before the earthquake, we had heard that a group of young people had gathered in the courtyard of the Cathedral to begin a three-day fast in protest at social injustices. They were protesting against malnutrition, the housing shortage, the exploitation of labour and the way the people are robbed and they had asked for a Christmas without political prisoners.

Rebecca speaks: "God chose from birth to live the same as the poorest, didn't he? Well, I don't think that God wants to see us stuffing ourselves with food and throwing money around, as Ernesto said, or to see trade doing well out of celebrating his birth. Perhaps he wants us to await his birth the way Nicaragua is now, because he was born poor and wants us all to be poor. Isn't that so? or rather he wants us all to be equal and doesn't

want us to do what was done in Managua, where Christmas was
only a feast for spending money (if you had any), and for enjoying yourself. They didn't celebrate Christ's coming as far as
I can see."

Another adds: "The Scriptures are clear enough. The fact
is that Christ was born poor, like the humblest of men. The
Scriptures tell us this and I don't see why we can't understand."

And someone else: "These things make us take stock, and
bring us closer to him. We've got off course, all of us, and we
need to be brought up against it to make us change our ways."

Pedro Rafael Gutiérrez is a Managua journalist who has been
with us for two months. He says: "I am really a stranger
among you (Cosme Canales brought me here in his motor-boat
exactly two months ago), but I feel a great affection for all of
you, for Octavio, Tomás Peña, Doña Justa, Laureano, Alejandro,
William, Tere and Ernesto, and I am sorry to leave you, now
that I'm going to the ruins of Managua to search for my family.
You really are poor, but believe me, I'm going to find people
there poorer than you, without water, light or food, even without a Communion like this one. If only this terrible grief in
Managua brings a new birth. Innocent people died in Managua,
as they died when Christ was born, but Christ lived, and that is
what matters. If only we can use this terrible Christmas there
to make a complete change. Good-bye to you all."

José the carpenter speaks next: "The change must be for
everybody. Among us as well, nobody must try to dominate anyone else. We have only just read about Jesus being born poor,
among the animals. He was born like that for a definite purpose. . . ."

Old Tomás Peña, who as well as being a farmworker is also
a fisherman: "To teach us not to go after riches, a big house
and then only one child in it, right? But to look for what is
natural."

I speak next, saying that Pedro was right to speak of this
anguished Christmas of Managua as a new birth. Christ at the
Last Supper spoke of his death as a birth. He said that a woman
suffers great pain when she is going to give birth, but afterwards
she rejoices when her son is born. That is how he explained his
own death and also the whole of human suffering. Women un-

derstand this better and his mother Mary would understand it very well, for she felt her pains in a stable at the first Christmas. Perhaps he said it specially for her, as she was to suffer so much at his passion, but he also said it for all of us. Human suffering has a meaning—it leads to birth.

One of the young men—Julio—speaks: "But perhaps the suffering of Managua is only going to be of use to the Christians, to those who understand. Perhaps it'll be no use for the others, who aren't going to understand it."

Another young man: "Suffering is for everybody, whether they understand it or not, and birth is for everybody, although perhaps Christians are the only ones who can understand suffering."

Felipe, the son of Tomás Peña, turns towards me and says: "I believe, Ernesto, that Jesus Christ has done this now, at Christmas, because he particularly likes us all to be equal. A lot of people in Managua meant to spend this Christmas enjoying themselves even though others were suffering; and if the tragedy had not been in Managua, if it had been in the countryside, they wouldn't be at all sad. But as it's Managua that was destroyed, now we are all living equality together, we all feel the suffering of all."

Pedro Rafael Gutiérrez, the journalist, speaks again: "What Felipe has said is beautiful. Christmas last year was a very happy Christmas in Managua. The rich had enormous turkeys, lovely Christmas trees and plenty of lights and decorations in their houses. But barrios like Acahualinca had nothing. There was worse poverty there than in the countryside. This year in Acahualinca they still haven't got anything, but the rich haven't either. Suffering has levelled us out. For the first time in the history of Nicaragua, rich and poor have shared suffering, which only the poor had before. And this is the most beautiful thing that has happened because suffering has brought us all together."

Alejandro, another of the young men: "One thing needs to be made clear. We are not going to celebrate because there was suffering for all. Best of all would be to have no one suffering, for everyone to have enough to be happy at Christmas time. I just thought that needed saying."

I tell them: "The goal is to overcome suffering and even

death. We Christians believe that one day death will be defeated (by life, that is by love). Even now we can triumph over illness, ignorance, poverty, and also over natural disasters, through love. As things are, we have a social system that cannot solve those problems. That city suffered a great misfortune with a selfish, individualist system in operation, which is what capitalism is; a system where everybody goes his own way and follows his own interests, and there is none of the union and co-operation that exists among certain animals such as the ants and the bees. In a society where there is solidarity instead of selfishness, men can protect themselves perfectly well from natural disasters like the eruption of a volcano, or an earthquake. Jesus came on earth precisely for this. He was born into a humanity divided and dominated by crime, to unite us and change this order of things. That's what we are talking about. . .".

Felix interrupts me: "I think the Managua business had to happen because of sin. . . ."

Oliva, Alejandro's mother: "The earthquake wasn't caused by sin. The consequences of the earthquake *are* due to sin, because selfishness is sin."

Julio: "Sufferings are not punishment from God, because the poor are the ones who suffer most. If you are rich you buy a car or a plane, and you get out of the city. You have no problem."

Another man adds: "I think that being rich is no use to anyone at the moment, even to the president: he loves his money, and as part of the presidential palace has collapsed, he feels that he's dying, when he isn't at all."

Pedro Rafael Gutiérrez speaks again: "I think the rich are the ones who are suffering most in this earthquake, and I'll tell you why: Acahualinca has never had water, light, milk, rice or beans. Now, this Christmas, the others haven't got them either. But for long enough the poor have been without food and without light, they've spent every Christmas like that. The radio speaks of people going out into the streets without shoes or clothes, but how long have the poor been without shoes or clothes?

"It's been like that since the time of Christ's birth. . . ."

Felix speaks again: "I'm going to tell you something. Listen,

Pedro. The rich never suffer. The government puts a five per cent tax on trade, but do the rich pay? No, the poor have to pay. And tell me—who are the workers of Nicaragua but the poor? Who really keeps trade going in Nicaragua? Isn't it the people who pay for it? And then this crisis comes and who gets fleeced to pay for it? Who else but us, the poor and the *campesinos* who work in Nicaragua?"

Outside there is a beautiful full moon, and the lake is calm on either side of the church. The young people are keeping up the dialogue now, almost by themselves.

"We aren't the only poor. Managua is full of poor people also, it isn't only the rich that are concentrated there, but most of the workers of the country also. And there are poor people everywhere."

"He came to share the lot of the poor. Joseph and Mary were turned away from the inn because they were poor. If they had been rich they would have been very well received."

"God wished his Son to be born in a cowshed, a stable. . . . He wanted his Son to belong to the poorer classes, didn't he? If God had wanted him to be born to a rich lady, she would have had her room fixed up in that hotel, especially arriving there pregnant."

"I see the humility of God in that. It was his Son, and he was born just like any dog is. Jesus came to liberate the world from these injustices (which continue to exist). He came so we would be united and would fight against these injustices. . . . Because we're still like this, with the boot on our necks. And how do the rich look on us? Always from above downwards. That's why we must unite to conquer, or rather we must all form a single revolutionary, like Christ. He was the greatest revolutionary, because being God, he became one with the poor, and came down from heaven to become one of the lower class, and he gave his life for us all. I think we must fight for others like that and be like him, unite and be brave. That way, nobody will be homeless and even if a man's house falls down because of an earthquake, he'll get it back again. And nobody will be ground down by the rich."

"With today's gospel, it seems to me that no poor man must undervalue himself. I think that it is obvious that a poor man is more important than a rich man. Christ is with us, the poor. I think we are worth more, for God, that is. For the rich, we are worth nothing except to work for them."

"God is teaching us also with this gospel, that the rich look on us as nothing, as if we have no value. For them, we don't even exist. Here we see that they treated his Son like that, they gave him no value at all, not even a canvas chair or a camp-bed to sleep in."

"The poor man supports the rich, because without his work they would be nothing. They don't realize that all they have is thanks to the poor. They think they get everything through their money, but it is through the poor, and of course when they have their banquets they don't bother about us. They think that their banquets are for themselves alone. They don't see that without us, they don't count either."

"Jesus was rejected in Bethlehem because he was poor, and he's still being rejected in the world for that same reason. In fact, the poor man is always rejected. In this system, I mean."

"But now, this Christmas, Managua is without houses, just as Jesus was born in Bethlehem without a house. And there are no Christmas banquets, just as when Jesus was born, there were no banquets in Bethlehem. Now, this Christmas appears to me to be more Christian, and may help to create more of a consci-ence about things and lead to everyone having a house, every-body being happy and nobody being rejected."

At the end, they talk about a collection for Managua. Some offer maize, others rice or beans. Felix asks me if I am going to Managua the next day. I tell him I will try to get there (I have no news of my family either) although I don't know if there is any transport.

"When there's no transport, your feet will have to do."

Translated by J. P. Donnelly

Dorothee Sölle and Fulbert Steffensky

Christianity as Joy in Sects and Fringe Groups

I. Church and Sect

IN his "National Anthem for Nicaragua" Ernesto Cardenal says, "There is so much maize to plant, so many children to teach, so many sick people to cure, so much love to create, so much poetry. My poem is about a land which will soon be born. The lake in some places blue, in others silver and gold; herons in the sky. Communism or the kingdom of God on earth, it's all the same. Tanks turned into tractors, police cars into school buses, and the machine will become man's best friend. . . . And I dream of the day when there will be no more rich people. But for today let us write these words on the walls: LIFE IS SUBVERSIVE or LOVE IS THE AGITATOR."[1]

This passage shows one modern attempt to express faith in terms of joy. It is not the literary product of an individual poet, but a poem "for" a people, a poem which cannot be understood without a knowledge of the context in which it was written.

The poem comes from a police state in Central America. The ruling clique of the Somozas, which itself owns a fifth of the land of the country, keeps itself in power by terror, torture and a system of informers. In Nicaragua life has to be "subversive", and love, if it intends to survive, cannot not "agitate". Cardenal is trying to live this subversive life in an agricultural commune on one of the islands of Lake Nicaragua. It is a Christian attempt to build an island of new life in the midst of the sea of the old.

[1] This is a prose rendering of a poem in Ernesto Cardenal's collection, *Oraculo sobre Managua* (Buenos Aires, 1973).

Islands of this sort, fringe groups, deviants, "sects", have always been part of the history of the Church, and are still part of it today. It is impossible to describe them without explaining the form of the Church to which they are in opposition. Sect and church are two mutually related forms of religion, two possible and necessary instances of the interpretation of faith. Viktor Ragaz calls the opposition one "between the static and the forward-thrusting form of religion", and talks about "an aesthetic and liturgical and an ethical and prophetic religious spirit".[2] Ernst Troeltsch made these two opposing movements part of his distinction between the organizational forms "church" and "sect". He refrained from a theological judgment on the two movements, and merely noted the different sociological effects of the gospel. A different approach is taken by the Marxist and non-theologian Konrad Farner, who describes the history of fringe groups in the Church as the most important and relevant "history of the great hope". "It is a completely new hope. It is particularly the hope of a quite small minority, a tiny, despised and persecuted group of alien origin. It is the certainty which proclaims all-embracing love, the equality of all men before death. . . . It is the confidence which means to do without violence, without material power, with only the power of the spirit."[3] This great hope of primitive Christianity is reformulated again and again in the history of the Church in the sects and fringe groups. Farner, like Troeltsch, contrasts it with the Church: "This institutionalized, established Church is— and has been throughout its history—only one part of Christianity, the static, cautious, largely backward-looking, socially conservative part. It has largely shed the great hope of eschatology, and brands all chiliasm as heresy, but its condemnations are not enough to put out the flames of revolt."

The Church history of the history books, which is the history of the Church as opposed to the sects, has neglected fringe groups or treated them only statistically or deterministically. By doing this it shows that it knows its master, whatever has prevailed and

[2] V. Ragaz, *Das Evangelium und der soziale Kampf der Gegenwart* (1906).
[3] Both this and the following quotation are taken from K. Farner, *Theologie des Kommunismus* (Frankfurt, 1969), p. 274.

come to power. Farner points out that this attitude to history equates the true with the strong and truth with power. But can such a view of history claim to be a true descendant of its founder, to go back to the powerlessness of Jesus of Nazareth and his truth?

This article will try to describe some of the features of the other Church, the secret one which has died out or gone underground, and explain its connection with the theme of joy.[4] We shall call fringe groups "sects," without implying that they are or were sects in the formal sense. Fringe groups can be found in the Church from the time of the primitive community, whose "church" counterpart was the Judaism of the time. Later examples are the early monastic movement, the Cathari, the Humiliati, the various groups among the Franciscans, the Waldensians, the groups around Wycliff and Hus, the Taborites and the Moravian Brethren, Müntzer and his peasants and the Anabaptist movements, the early Pietist groups, down to modern groups like that around the Berrigan brothers in the United States or Don Mazzi and his group in Isolotto in Florence.

These sects share a number of common features:

1. They are in relation to the Church. They are connected with it, persecuted by it, explicitly tolerated by it, tamed by it. This means that they do not include groups like the Jehovah's Witnesses, whom we commonly call sects, and which at the time of their secession may have had the characteristics of a sect but have long since acquired "church" features.

2. The Church claims for itself, and denies to the sects, the unique competence to preach the true gospel and to give instruction in true Christian life.

3. These groups are not purely dogmatic secessions (like the Arians). They are not groups with a special doctrine, related only to the theological superstructure; what is more important is their different way of life, their different Christian *praxis*.

[4] The authors of this essay are indebted to Troeltsch, but recognize his weaknesses. Troeltsch combined individual features of different sects to produce a general picture, an ideal type of the sect, without subjecting his model to sufficient empirical verification.

4. Sects have a specifically radical quality, which can be explained by group psychology as a result of their relation as a small group to a large one. This quality includes intensity, sharp conflicts, rigorism towards their own members as well as towards the Church. Theologically, however, which means as regards content, this is not all.

II. THE INFINITIVE PASSION

The Christian faith can be described as an infinite passion, a passion for life that increases the intensity of both our pleasure and our pain. The tendency common to all religions to reject banality—and according to Isaak Babek banality is the counter-revolution!—reaches an extreme in Christianity. Faith is a firm refusal to allow banality to gain power over us, a refusal which leads at times to extremes and threatens to shatter communication with other people. This sense of pathos in life, this emphasis, frees both pleasure and pain from their limits and intensifies them; they become deprivatized and largely detached from their specific causes. Pleasure makes itself independent; it in particular has the capacity to go beyond its object and become 'itself alone'.

The older language expressed this very directly by connecting "pleasure" with the preposition "in" ("Joy is in thee"), or using it absolutely and emphatically ("joy, joy upon joy"), without feeling a need to mention the reason. You could say that you found pleasure or were pleased "in" God; to say that one was pleased "about" him would be too slight, a merely partial expression, turning God into a function when he is incommensurable even with the totality of pleasure. The happiness that can say, "I have pleasure in you," has the boundlessness of an ocean; the heart "swims" in pleasure without reaching the end. One criterion of the truth of pleasure is the part sexuality has in its expression. An asexual language of pleasure, a pleasure which is only felt "about" something, but not "in" someone, should make us suspicious. A pleasure that retains in its language nothing of pushing one's way in, pouring oneself out, conceiving, being born, floating, physical pleasure, is itself only a partial and therefore repressive language, and has not yet reached the totality implied by the expression "delighting in God".

It is characteristic of the sects that their pleasure, like their pain, claims that extreme of completeness which, in delight about this or that, experiences delight in God. Lovers of God share in his delights.

Because the relations between members of a small group are more intensive, communication and participation in such a group are almost continuous. This results in a different experience of life—more pleasure, more excitement, more expression. In the same way asceticism within the sects is not a means to sanctification or a special morality practised by particular groups; it is what makes possible the fellowship of all in love, and is practised by all members of the sect alike. It becomes an instrument in the service of pleasure.

The lovers of God share in his delights. When a new child is born it is not just a happiness and an enrichment for the family, nor just a natural event; the child belongs to the group, is experienced by the group as a new source of riches; the God of the group grows and becomes stronger. Similarly, the pain of such a group is always pain that the kingdom of God has not yet come, pain at each new delay or destruction of it. For such a group, the destruction of the hope for democratic socialism in Chile means a defeat that affects the whole pattern. The "land which will soon be born", about which all fringe groups have songs, is now further away; the colours of the lake, the symbols of infinite happiness, are now darkened. Pleasure and pain are related to a total pattern in which we have a part, which does not leave us out.

III. HUMANISTIC AND AUTHORITARIAN RELIGION

This religious experience of unity with the whole, which involves greater joy and greater vulnerability, is characteristic of only one type of religion, "humanistic" as opposed to "authoritarian" religion. This distinction, first made by Erich Fromm, cuts across the traditional distinctions between religions, such as that between theistic and non-theistic. Authoritarian religion is the recognition of a higher invisible power which can demand obedience, reverence and worship. God is a powerful authority; man powerless and insignificant: "The experience ... of despising everything in oneself ... is the very essence of authoritarian religions.... Man's worth consists in the very denial of his worth and strength."[5] On this view the essential feature of authoritarian religion is subjection to a power outside men, and the chief virtue is consequently obedience.

Humanistic religion, in which Fromm includes early Buddhism, Taoism, the teaching of Isaiah, Jesus, Socrates and Spinoza, certain strands in Judaism and Christianity (especially mysticism) and the religion of reason in the French Revolution, is centred on man and his strength. "The prevailing mood is ... joy, while the prevailing mood in authoritarian religion is ... sorrow and guilt."[6] The goal of such religions is that man should attain his greatest strength, not his greatest weakness. Virtue in this case is self-realization, not obedience.

The relationship between humanistic and authoritarian religion cannot be simply transferred to that between sects and churches. The churches have a share of humanistic elements, handed down by tradition, and the fringe groups are threatened by new authority structures. Nevertheless it can be shown that in all sects the mood of joy and unity prevails over that of guilt and fear. The place of obedience as the main virtue is undermined by the rejection of the authority of the churches. Its symbols—such as purgatory—are deprived of importance. The rejection of the objective institutional nature of the Church leads to the rejection or relativization of the priesthood and of hierarchical distinctions. (All reform movements within the Catholic Church have begun with a relativization of the priesthood.) Against a collective identity in an objectively institutional Church, administered by officials and based on a sacramental and legal structure, the sects insist on individual Christianity.

The criticism is directed equally against control by Church or State. The Waldensians, for example, condemned and rejected both the laws of the Empire and canon law. According to a prayer of the Cathari, Lucifer, the devil, said that it was right

---

[5] Erich Fromm, *Psychoanalysis and Religion* (New Haven, Conn., 1958), p. 36.
[6] Fromm, p. 37.

"for one to oppress others with his orders", and that "there should be those who became kings, lords or emperors, and used one bird to catch another and one beast to catch another".[7] It is a joke from the garden of Eden against the structure of domination.

The rejection of authorities is based on a new assessment of protology and eschatology. According to Troeltsch, the Church starts from relative natural law, post-fall natural law. The world is fallen, and man is regarded as evil, and therefore various forms of authority are necessary: the power of the State, law, force, oaths and war, the distinction between man and woman, poor and rich. In other words, nature is fallen, including man's nature, which has to be hedged about with so many institutions. Churches are always ready to compromise with the present. They are adaptable; they accept new discoveries and new systems of thought, and adapt themselves to them. Eschatology counts for very little.

With the sects it is different. They are not interested in dominating the world, but in reducing its importance in relation to a better future. The world of the beginning and the world of the end have the same structure, and this is directly normative for the here and now. For the sects paradise and the kingdom of God are not just a vague memory and a distant promise, but a pattern and a guide to action. "When Adam delved and Eve span, who was then the gentleman," sang the peasants in the Reformation period. Sects appeal to absolute natural law. In paradise there was neither State nor oath, therefore any oath is to be rejected, "however honestly and justly it is sworn". In paradise there were no superiors and no private property, neither the limited distinction between man and woman nor that between rich and poor. This means that women have the right to preach and uneducated people to expound Scripture.

The memory of an undestroyed world in which there was no domination is central for the sects; it is their ground for relegating all distinctions to secondary status or demanding their abolition. They reject the willingness of the churches to compromise and their tendencies to adaptation, and try to assert the laws of

[7] Quoted from H. J. Schulz (ed.), *Die Wahrheit der Ketzer* (Stuttgart, 1968), pp. 242, 257, 259.

the beginning and the end. Where this is impossible they insist on strict separation from the world. The oppositions between the world of the beginning and the present world are absolute. Like all value-orientated groups, sects cannot make gradations in the structure of the world or in their assessments. They think in dichotomies and absolute opposites. Their picture of themselves is based on their picture of the enemy. They try to implement the absolute laws of the origin and the end in their own group or to extend them to everyone. Wherever possible, fringe groups insist on strict separation from the world.

In a talk given in the autumn of 1973, Ernesto Cardenal said, "It is impossible to be a Christian within the capitalist system. You have to isolate yourself." When asked how this could be done, he talked about the reversal of values and abandonment of the values of capitalism. Christianity, understood as a humanistic religion, needs isolation, not as an escape from the world or mere regression, but for the sake of its own identity.

IV. THE END OF EXTERNAL CONTROL

Joy or pleasure can become the prevailing religious mood when external control is removed. The rejection of external control is an important topic in all reports about heretics. The intensity of individual Christianity prevails over ritualized magical practices.

Seen as part of the history of religion, rationality or mystical intensity appears as destructive of practices. The reports of the Inquisition dwell at remarkable length on the way sects destroy the obligatory division of the world into holy places, times, persons and actions often practised in churches.

The following passage occurs in a report from 1398 about Waldensians in Austria:

"They believe that a cemetery is no holier than a field or any other piece of ground. They think that a church is no holier than an ordinary house. They regard a consecrated altar as no holier than any pile of stones. They say that the wood of the holy cross is no holier than any ordinary piece of timber, and think the same of the crown of thorns. They think the same of the iron nails in the hands and feet of Christ and of the table on which Jesus instituted the sacrament. They think the same of the Holy Land of Jerusalem, of Bethlehem, Nazareth and other holy places."

We have quoted this at length because it typifies the sects' attacks on the repressive character of gestures and rituals, against the compulsion inherent in a life based on them. The churches were remarkably sensitive to these infringements of their rules.

Even the reports left by the Inquisitors about the heretics convey a feeling of almost physical pleasure in the destruction of continuing external control. In details the attack on the solidity of sacramentalism shows an element of fun; the destruction of the symbols of the Church confirmed the sects' own rejection of imposed external control.

"The singing in God's Church is not pleasing to God. The prayers said in churches for the dead are of no value to them. The blessed virgin and the other saints in heaven cannot intercede for men on earth."

A report of the Inquisition of about 1390 states that the Waldensians were able to create their own sacraments and administer them to their people. The importance of the minister was reduced; any form of domination, whether by force, knowledge or consecration, was rejected and its symbols mocked or destroyed. This is another feature which can be followed down to the present. In Maryland, Philip Berrigan poured blood over the draft cards, and later Philip and Dan burned the archive in Catonsville with napalm they had made themselves out of detergent and petrol. During a tourist tour of the White House, a young woman belonging to the same group around the American Thomas Merton Center poured blood over Nixon's dining-room table. In fiction Heinrich Böll has created a similar symbol in *End of a Mission*: an army jeep is drenched with petrol and burnt. These are practical jokes turned into dramatizations of liberation, new acts of piety which symbolize the rejection of the values of the dominant system.

With this rejection of inauthentic life there goes a new sense of being chosen. New values appear which contradict the prevailing norms. One of the main values of the sects has always been poverty. It is a value in a double sense. On the one hand, the reduction of the importance of the world makes people more independent, less enslaved, and on the other the wish to share everything and to want nothing for oneself is the political motive for poverty. The same motive is present in Don Mazzi's group in Isolotto, and the attempt of the priests involved in it to abandon a middle-class existence has been felt—as such attempts are felt in all periods—as an attack on the hierarchy. When Mazzi turned his spacious presbytery into an orphanage, this was regarded as breaking the rules. The tendency to vegetarianism to be seen in many American groups also corresponds to a rejection of this capitalist world, in which social and assumed sexual potency is co-ordinated with the size of the steaks ("as rare as possible") consumed each day.

These characteristics would be wrongly classified if they were regarded as a rejection of sensuality. Among heretics and fringe groups sensuality has always been acute, for example in a new capacity for and pleasure in perception. An example is Francis's attitude to fire. When his hut burned down and his sheepskin was saved, he would never again wear it because it had been "snatched from Brother Fire". Another story draws attention to the connection of fire and pleasure. While Francis and Clare were having a pleasant time together, the people in the neighbourhood suddenly saw the wood and the monastery burst into flames. They rushed up in horror to put out the fire only to find a cheerful group sitting around a simple meal. They then realized that the fire was the fire of divine love, with which the souls of the holy brothers and sisters were ablaze. This new valuation of "Brother Fire" points towards a new form of sensuality; it would be impossible in a church with a carefully graded system even for the emotion it tolerates. The representative of a hierarchical system cannot permit or wish his scorched linen trousers to be left as a present to Brother Fire and not extinguished. This different attitude to money or goods is a joke which is also an act of liberation.

V. NEW WAYS OF USING THE BIBLE

Churches and sects differ in the ways they use the Bible, and first of all in what they select and admit. The churches use mainly the Pauline letters, the fringe groups the preaching of Jesus, which they regard as the law of life. For the churches, the Bible is a redemptive institution which confers reassurance and comfort on the individual. For the fringe groups it is relevant in a quite different way, as a guide to action. Without any deep reflection, scriptural sayings are set down one after the other, as in the rules of the Franciscans, and the sayings about taking nothing on one's journey, welcoming guests and, above all, poverty are taken as simple, easily intelligible and clear instructions. Where churches use the Decalogue as a milder code of conduct, sects choose the Sermon on the Mount.

The way the Bible is used in relation to action itself produces a different community structure. Instructions for action which remain inadequate, unclear or anonymous have a tendency to intensify depressive states. The Church's main interest is not in guidance for action, which is usually derived for the most part from a general world-view and brought into conformity with existing values. As a result it usually appears as anonymous and unclear. The Church's real interest is in the complicated intellectual procedures of theology; study, interpretation and strict systematization contribute to building up a theory which has no clear relevance to action. Even the best theology in the Church therefore becomes an elitist science, i.e., one which supports domination. In this context we can understand the Waldensians' advice to "condemn and reject all privileged studies".

In the Church, the Bible is not used as a guide to action; indeed, it is not allowed to have this function. The Church was much more interested in protecting people from the Bible or encouraging them to understand it within a few specified contexts. In the sects, on the other hand, interpretation was performed by all; a sort of "wild-cat" exegesis was the rule, something like what is attempted today in small Christian groups, or the dominant approach in the Isolotto catechism. The aim is not historical, which also means distancing, knowledge to provide comfort and distraction as part of a complex cognitive system, but rather immediate application, which recognizes the crucified Jesus in napalm victims.

This direct relation with the origin of the faith is guided mainly by the exhortatory passages of Scripture. The relevance of church attitudes to action is slight, but those of the sects, on the other hand, have a strong tendency to take active forms. As the ramifications of the intellectual system become more complex, as in contemporary university theology, which is under pressure to prove itself a science, the less capable it is of giving rise to action. This incapacity is explained in Protestantism with the argument that our strength and our works are "worthless", but its practical effect is to thrust people into uncertainty, doubt and depression. The ramifications of a church official's thinking, combined with a totally secure existence, can never produce a Christianity which sees itself as based on joy.

In the small group, on the other hand, the goals—such as the banning of genocide—are clearly seen, and the whole group co-operates in looking for appropriate behaviour and developing it into a strategy. The clarity about what is to be done now which is thus produced is one precondition for joy. A person's identity is not isolated, nor its exercise indefinitely postponed, but brought to life. Sects are carried along by a sort of anthropological optimism, a trust in "people", who are good, and in the power of the Spirit, while the churches tend to adopt a pessimistic view of individuals and the people. In the eyes of the Church, the people need leadership, and movements within it are suspect. The conflict between the Cardinal of Florence and Don Mazzi shows this alignment of attitudes as clearly as any Reformation dispute. Müntzer said that it was the Spirit of Christ, "destined to be the mockery and downfall of our scholars", who led the people. One of Luther's charges against Müntzer was that he taught "the stable boys in the country to say mass". This trust in the people and the power of the Spirit usually only lasts until the leader has formed his own organization, however. The optimism of a Rousseau can exist only before the success of the revolution, and afterwards Hobbesian pessimism returns. This certainly gives us cause for thought.

VI. Identity and Joy

There can be no joy unless a person is sure of his identity. The complex intellectual system of the churches dare not rely on the ability of individuals to make decisions for themselves, and this is why it is satisfied with a natural way of incorporating its members, i.e. infant baptism. Sects, on the other hand, are voluntary associations and require deliberate adherence; a baptismal certificate gives no guarantee of admission. Consequently, all sects have either rejected infant baptism or reduced its importance, and required a second, spiritual baptism. When the churches' sacramentalism obscures individual participation or makes it unnecessary, Christian fringe groups make the responsible individual the centre of their beliefs. In the place of a standardized identity they assert the identity of the particular individual. They abandon the world of unthinking sacramentalism and hierarchical structures, and the members of the new group acquire security from their awareness of being specially chosen and from the brotherly relationships between them. A new sort of simplicity comes into existence, free from the burden of theology and its alien impositions.

This tendency to simplicity shows itself in the present in attempts to find ways of living without complex technological apparatus. For American groups, for example, relationships with nature and natural products are very important—homemade bread, for example, has become a new symbol. A person's identity is no longer expressed in the socially recognized symbols and values (car, job, position in an occupational hierarchy with sharp distinctions above and below), but in new symbols and gestures. The eucharist is celebrated with people sitting on the floor singing protest songs. The celebrants are people wanted by the FBI, who are just out of prison or likely to be imprisoned. The joy of having to suffer is part of the great joy, of a life which is subversive.

Translated by Francis McDonagh

Norbert Schiffers

The Humour of John XXIII

THE thousands who attended papal audiences were familiar with
the kindly, keenly observant eyes which flashed over the rims
of Pope John's spectacles when he wanted to make a point. Like
all Italians, when he spoke Giovanni acted out the punctuation
of his text with his eyes. His right eyebrow and the corners of
his mouth would be slightly raised when what he was saying
was not just a prepared text but came from his heart. At such
moments Papa Roncalli looked amused. Even the *Daily Express*,
hardly a pro-Catholic paper, commented: "The first jolly Pope".

I. Conditions

But this John was not always light-hearted. It took particular
conditions to kindle his cheerfulness. John the cleric needed
visual contact with those he talked to in order to argue at his
ease. Only in direct conversation did he really answer questions.
Questions from his companions, and also questions which came
into his own mind when he noticed to his surprise that other
people were not just different people, but had different expectations. Immediately after his election, when all the papal cassocks
carefully tailored for possible candidates proved far too tight, the
unexpected winner joked, "They all wanted me except the
tailors!" The surprise of those who had expected a different
pope turned into a question in his own mouth. "Who knows",
he is reported as saying at his first blessing from the balcony,

"whether all the people down there wanted me, when they didn't elect me?"

The first condition evoking humour was questions from a contact group.

Pope John welcomed questions. They clearly did not disturb him, not even the questions of experts. In his *Journal of a Soul* he records that as his text for meditation in his exercises in the late autumn of 1940 he chose Psalm 51, the *Miserere*. As a help in interpretation he used a commentary by an exegete of whom he thought highly, Father Segneri. Under 29 November Roncalli notes, speaking of the fifteenth verse of the psalm, "Dear Fr Segneri has spent fifteen pages of commentary on this verse. He says many beautiful things, but to me they smack too much of baroque verbosity. For me the interpretation is much more simple and practical.... I consider myself." The entry is informative. "Dear Fr Segneri's" questions were noted, but the answer is not derived from the text, from specialist exegesis. Roncalli looks for the answer in himself as an antithesis. Other people's questions, collected in complicated bundles, weighed out and still not offering any decision, become a stimulus which enables him to find a simple and therefore practical answer for himself. Roncalli (and Pope John too) made decisions like the peasants, simply, practically, naïvely convincing. What is practical is always simple, but simplicity is only realistic when it is based on a conviction which has stood the test of experience.

Humour grows—this is the second condition—only out of a person's own experience and a habit of making decisions simply.

John the Pope had an eye for surprising decisions. He was longsighted (the reason why he wore glasses), which prevented him from being absorbed, like his advisers, in historical or theoretical objections, which the nervous saw at every turn. He never went close to the wall to feel it for chinks and weaknesses. Looking into the distance, he saw solutions to problems which took by surprise the specialists hunched over the object. Giovanni did not patch holes with pages out of textbooks. He went back to the fruits of existential experience and tried out what had worked for him in a different situation as a general solution. John's solutions were different from, and more surprising than, those of his predecessor Pius, who still thought in a scholastic way. "*Ecco,* that's it," Giovanni used to joke with a laugh. "Holy Father," asked Pius's cardinals, "why have this dangerous Council?" John left the questioners gasping for breath, opened the windows and let in fresh air. "That's why," he laughed. A cardinal of the Curia who had learnt the mental habits of the Pius era and had got used to being surprised summed up expectations and consternation in the remark: "Pius XII was a great mind, John XXIII has a great heart." Capovilla, the papal secretary, was blunter: "The Pope has no time for regrets about the past. He wants to bridge the gaps."

3   The third condition necessary to produce solutions which are humorous in their unexpectedness can be summed up in the principle that the memory of success lends distance to the problem and with it an ability to see solutions.

The work of John the pontiff, the bridge-builder, was always done, well in advance, in his own mind before the Pope opened his mouth. John did not suffer from the sort of crisis of identity which drives some people to put on an act whenever they say anything and leaves them looking inadequate rather than convincing. Said the Pope cheerfully, "My liver is sound and I have no trouble with my nerves. So I simply enjoy being with people." John knew that he surprised cautious thinkers. With his answers of one and two syllables ("Why?"—"That's why" or, to a seven-year-old blind boy, "Sometimes we are all blind"). He tried not only to get to the heart of situations, but also to get through to his own heart and those of others. These attempts gave him pleasure, the pleasure of a person who is self-assured, the satisfaction of someone who has put humbug behind him, the strong personality's experience of success.

Enjoyment, pleasure and experience free of resentment (all combined) are the chief conditions under which John XXIII's humour came to life.

Giovanni had a humour which could switch circuits out of old patterns into new ones. John had a trust in others and in himself which his biographers could not account for. The experiences which nourished this trust he normally kept to himself. He did not put his soul on show. Indeed he often concealed the seriousness of his ideas under wisecracks which were more like irony than humour. It is said that at the beginning of 1959, as he read the fifth Roncalli biography, he said, "They're all quite nice and even interesting. But one thing about all of them—they have very little or nothing to do with me." Pope John had not formally thought out what was important to him, but lived it out as the man Angelo Roncalli. With his own resources he had to see and decide what would work. And yet he was never a lonely nuncio, patriarch or pope. The confidence derived from his own experience and the seriousness of the humorous was combined in him with an irony that made it possible for him to say serious things.

Without irony John's humour would have been too heavy.

When he did not recite a prepared text but put forward his own ideas, he surprised his audiences. When their surprise showed him that the others had thought differently, but could still laugh with him and think about his ideas, he knew: "Now I have bridged a gulf." Capovilla remarked of this bridge-building humour that the Pope "tries to bridge gaps. He works for unity." From his experience, with his humour, John drew the motto which was only too often observed by no one but him, "bend, not break". The Italian word which sums up this well-considered surprise which can be achieved by someone who allows himself to be surprised by the unusual is *aggiornamento*. The attitude of *aggiornamento* does not exclude what is new and surprising (even if it is insoluble like the blindness of a boy who has to look forward to a life of blindness, does not miss it out, but treats it as a sign on a journey). In a heavy explanation of the meaning of his *aggiornamento*, John the preacher said, "Man's life is a journey towards eternity, towards heaven. We should think carefully as we go on this journey so that bliss may be never-ending."

Humour, and this is the last condition, does not take away the importance of the new which, because it is new, is unpleasant. Even if its importance means that we have to adapt to it.

II. LIMITATIONS

One limitation which not even humour can get beyond is the usual language of preaching. Anyone who has learnt to appreciate the surprising turns in John's humour will find passages like the one just quoted terrible, with their impersonal would-be universal validity and use of abstractions such as "life", "heaven", "bliss". Why not "my life" and "your life", "you and I", as we would expect from a witty person drawing insights from his own experience, instead of such banalities? No one is moved by language which sticks to abstract vocabulary, falls back on such worn images, which speak to literary training rather than experience. Their action is on the intelligence which merely records, and is therefore weary, and rejects the message because it has heard it all before. Many people in the past, reading "purple passages" like this, or even the well-intentioned paragraphs of Pope John's encyclicals, asked where Giovanni's humour had got to when Giovanni spoke or wrote in papal language. Did the office scare him? There are signs that it did. For example, on his Christmas visit in 1958 he said to an orphan boy called Angelo, "I used to be called Angelo too, but now they've given me another name." Behind the joke this remark says that the other, the papal, name, by which "they" addressed the office-holder, remained foreign to him. When Pope John had to act officially, it was as though Angelo's humour were blown away. His speeches, at least in the cleaned-up versions printed by the *Osservatore*, were as dry as papal speeches always have been. Pope John's encyclicals are curial, and so general in their language that they go quite well as footnotes in council documents.

To see this in John is symptomatic. It shows us something about what humour can do. Humour also has its limitations. It is only with very great writers, for example (such as Chesterton, perhaps), that written texts are sensitive enough to let the occasional genuinely funny remark slip through. Lesser men come a long way behind these great ones. Any lesser man who writes about the humour of John XXIII is struck by the humourlessness of what he writes. Is this weakness perhaps the result of a feeling that on record objective correctness is more important than conviction or honesty? Pope John, who was editor of a paper himself in Bergamo, is reported as having remarked, in reply to a question at a meeting with journalists, "Well, as shall we say a semi-professional, I know that journalists make the odd slip now and then." "The odd slip" introduces a personal observation into the objectifying text. Generally, though, the courage to make personal assessments, telling judgments, was crushed by the obligation to record only objective facts—except when humour risked an epigram. When he wrote John XXIII lost the boldness which prompted his humour and which was so natural to him when speaking.

One limitation of humour is writing.

The second limitation of humour is the masses.

Out of consideration for the crowds that wanted to see him, John allowed himself, in spite of his own reluctance, to be continued to be carried into St Peter's on the *sedia gestatoria*. Not openly, but only to the bearers, with whom he got on well, he joked about himself and the traditional apparatus: "The bobbing up and down on this rocking-horse makes me really giddy." Ideas which could have done away with traditional practices which were impractical for those involved were limited by the needs of the masses. The only exception was when along with the ideas he acquired the courage to use his own weaknesses as arguments against the claims of the masses. Humour made use of objections from experience.

Consideration for the needs of the masses is the end of joking, and indicates one limitation of humour.

The biggest obstacle to humour was the traditional dignity of the office. Even the new Pope, with long experience of being a dignitary, could not at first get to sleep until he jokingly told himself, "Giovanni, don't take yourself so seriously!" Because he could do this, he managed not to become a monument, with a plinth inscribed "Pope of the Council". Even during his lifetime he could explain the official "PP" after his signature, with a grin, as "Partito Popolare". He could not, however, achieve the more important, because continuing, result; he, the Pope on the side of the people, was unable to change the literary and administrative style of his Vatican. Official styles resist even the onslaughts of humour.

Official posts are barriers to humour, which let through only the official, not the personal side of the man who holds the position.

III. Effects

For John XXIII, attention to correctness in texts, to the wishes of the masses and to traditional demands of his office acted as limitations which kept his humour in check. Outside these areas there can be no doubt that John was witty. This is confirmed by the way his jokes won the devotion and even enthusiasm of ordinary people. We are left with a question. Can we learn anything from John's dilemma, "objects or people in the Church?"

I think we can, and it goes like this. Humour as a sign of a human Church is not to be expected from writers, from the impersonal masses, and not from official implementers of correct (conciliar) decisions. When correctness and appeals to the needs of the masses become priorities for action, humour dies. But, when there are people who have the gift, humour can make headway, move and humanize, in small groups. Independent experience, surprising recollections, pleasure in joy and a dash of irony, all the ingredients of humour, can only exist in groups which allow personal contact. What we lack, what we must try to create, are solidarity groups, small parishes. They would not have to work stolidly against the trend; it would be far more important, at least at first, that they should know how to live together. In living groups the Church could become more humorous, more human. This humour—as Pope John showed—would enable office-holders and a little later even the theologians dedicated to their books to make contact with the simple people, the base. For the important thing, the memory of God in the man Jesus, to get through to the base in the Church, what is needed is not orthodox leaders, but human beings who do not lose their humour. It should be a humour that can say illuminating things in surprising ways from personal experience, and not just in the traditional way, out of books. This sort of humour lives in small groups.

The legacy of the twenty-third John, the gift of his humour, remains with the groups at the base. But even these cells of the Church must take care not to revere their Pope with the longing of those who imagine that the human element in the Church has disappeared; they must not treat him as a monument of humour. In 1963, when he was dying, John told his household, "Don't worry so much about me. I'm ready. My bags are packed, and I can go at any time."

Angelo Giovanni went and took his humour with him. Our task is to let humour live. The humour of John who had the courage to trust will continue to be felt and leave its mark on the Church, but only in groups which are the expression, not of texts or monuments or offices, but of human beings and their experiences.

On 7 September 1900 Angelo Roncalli wrote in his diary, "Not bad on the whole". Perhaps he will have contributed enough humour to an arid account to make at least a few humorous readers say the same.

Translated by Francis McDonagh

Andrew Greeley

Humour and Ecclesiastical Ministry

AT the conclusion of his movie, *Roma,* Federico Fellini presents an "ecclesiastical fashion show." It is a bitter but uproariously funny satire on ecclesiastical dress and manners. One suspects that in particular Fellini has in mind the garb and custom of the Roman Curia. The scenes are very nasty (one would probably have to be Roman to appreciate how nasty), but they are also extremely humorous (and one would probably have to be Roman to appreciate how humorous). Some dismiss the fashion show as irreverent, others have suggested that it is blasphemous. Certainly the apparent ridicule of the long-dead Pius XII may be in questionable taste. But the relationship between Italian creative artists and the Vatican is so complex that those of us who are outsiders probably ought to be wary before passing judgment on the dialogue between those two curious sparring partners.

Why is the ecclesiastical fashion show so funny? It is much easier to laugh at something than to explain afterwards why it is amusing. But there seems to be two components in the humour of Fellini's satire. First in our twentieth-century North Atlantic culture it seems extraordinarily incongruous to see men parading around in such elaborate, colourful, and jewelled finery. Perhaps there is an implication in the Fellini film that since the ecclesiastical bureaucrats are celibate, they are not real men. There may be a touch of the vicious humour attending the transvestite, men dressing up like women.

The second element of the humour in the fashion show may be the incongruity of men supposedly dedicated to serving the poor and needy, supposedly preaching the gospel of "one who had not a place whereon to lay his head," appearing in expensive, ornate, and elaborate costumes, and marching around as though they were Byzantine potentates. There is, of course, caricature and exaggeration in this humour. However elaborate ecclesiastical dress may be, it is not so elaborate as that worn by Fellini's models. But the caricature makes its point: the solemn, pretentious, overly decorated ecclesiastical bureaucracy is wildly incongruous when compared to the message of the gospel.

At the conclusion of another bitterly anticlerical Italian movie, *The Priest's Wife*, we see a similar procession of ecclesiastical dignitaries. The satire here is not surrealistic but grimly realistic: fat, gross, smug, corrupt ecclesiastics march in solemn procession after having seduced the priest away from his "wife" by a promise of ecclesiastical advancement. To the theme of incongruity in Fellini's *Roma*, *The Priest's Wife* adds hypocrisy. This new theme is funnier and considerably more bitter.

Satire of the ecclesiastical ministry is by no means limited to the anticlericalism of Italian film-makers. Such diverse French writers as Gide, Bernanos, and Mauriac engaged in anticlerical satire. And there is bitter laughter at the expense of the ministry (combined with profound respect for the priesthood) in Graham Greene's *The Power and the Glory* and in his more recent *The Honorary Consul*. Trollope's novels show that satire of the clergy is by no means limited to Roman Catholics, although the Anglican parsons of the Barchester series are assailed by a satire that is neither so heavy as Greene's nor so acid as the continental writers.

And yet another style of ecclesiastical satire can be found among Irish writers in both Ireland and the United States. Indeed, it seems almost impossible for an Irish writer to produce a novel in which some kind of priestly character—malign or benign—does not appear. Of all the traditions of satire of the clergy the Irish may be the most powerful. The continentals simply hate their clergy; the Irish love them and hate them at the same time. This ambivalence produces figures of satire that are at once more human and more humorous. The master of ecclesiastical satire is the American writer J. F. Powers. He may be the funniest of all because he is the gentlest of all. He is gentle because he has the most profound understanding of the incongruity—hence the humour—of any man's frailties, weaknesses, and limitations, especially of those who pretend to represent the Deity.

Ecclesiastical satire as humour is ancient. It surely goes back as far as Chaucer and Dante and, further, to Aristophanes' comic treatment of the oracles. In the Irish tradition, the chronicles of the very early Middle Ages abound with ecclesiastical humour.[1] As displeasing as it may be to ecclesiastical authorities, there seems little likelihood that such humour will ever stop. Only when such worthies cease to fall so ludicrously short of their ideals will there be nothing left to satirize. Only when ecclesiastical office and responsibility cease to dispose the all too fragile human personalities to pomposity, fake, pretence and hypocrisy will the opportunity for and the need of ecclesiastical satire end. It may be nasty and vicious, but there is no way to escape it. Indeed, I think, as a product of the Irish tradition, that ecclesiastical satire is more effective when viciousness is replaced by wry, gentle irony of the J. F. Powers sort. *Morte d'Urban* is funnier than Fellini's ecclesiastical fashion show, and it is more effective as satire. There is, however, room for both.

Ecclesiastics may continue to rail against those who poke fun at them, but that will not stop the laughter. Priests, religious and bishops are funny—all human beings are funny, but ecclesiastics are somehow funnier. The Lord Jesus did indeed say something about using the foolish in this world to confound the wise.

[1] "Now two maidens with pointed breasts used to lie with him (the monk Scuthian) every night, that the battle with the Devil might be the greater for him. And it was proposed to accuse him on that account. So Brenainn (St Brendan) came to test him, and Scuthian said: "Let the cleric lie in my bed tonight," saith he. So when he reached the hour of resting the girls came into the house wherein was Brenainn ... and go into bed to him.... They lie down with Brenainn, and nowise could he sleep with longing. "That is imperfect, O cleric," say the girls; "he who is here every night feels nothing at all. Why goest thou not, O cleric, into the tub (of cold water) if it be easier for thee? 'Tis often that the cleric, even Scuthian, visits it." "Well," says Brenainn, "it is wrong for us to make this test, for he is better than we are." (Vivian Mercier, *The Irish Comic Tradition,* Oxford, 1962, p. 46).

The tale has been retold in modern Irish ecclesiastical circumstances by George Moore in his book *A Storyteller's Holiday.* Scuthian becomes a parish priest, Brendan, a bishop's secretary from the chancery office.

There are times, however, when he seems to have carried the foolishness theme just a bit too far.

There are two other kinds of religious humour: the humour of the sacred and the humour of faith. Both are related to ecclesiastical satire, but they have their own unique style and purpose. No one has ever participated in an elaborate ecclesiastical ceremonial who could claim that he never felt the urge to laugh. Indeed, it is usually at the most solemn moments of the ceremony that the urge is strongest. All that is required is for someone to make a mistake—sing a wrong note, bow in the wrong direction, kiss the wrong ring, bring the wrong utensil, doff the wrong biretta, make the wrong turn, ring the wrong bell—and all present are swept with waves of merriment.

It seems unconscionable, sacrilegious, blasphemous, but it is funny and the more we try to pretend it's not, the funnier it gets.

When I was in the seminary one of the priests who came periodically to propose points for meditation for night prayers was obsessed with the evils of "levity," as he called it. By this he meant laughter in chapel during mass or vespers. But his jeremiads against levity were extraordinarily funny. We would come into the chapel in the evening, see him kneeling in the back and begin to laugh on our way to the pews. We were sorry, we didn't mean to laugh and we knew our laughter would distress him, to say the least. Still, the very sight of that intense, rigid figure preparing to inveigh against levity was unbearably funny. Surely we knew it was risky to anger this powerful man, and we would much have preferred not to, but there was nothing for it—he was funny, and we had to laugh.

It was also thought proper in those dim, pre-Vatican II days, to check early in the week to see who the cantors at vespers would be. Everyone had a pretty good idea of the chanting ability of everyone else. The whole week would be spent in delighted anticipation of a particularly bad singer due to appear with a particularly difficult set of antiphons. We approached Sunday vespers, it must be confessed, in expectation of marvellous merriment. (I must confess, as one of the worst singers of my era, that I was not always amused.)

Why do we have this impulse to laugh at the most solemn

and sacred times? My guess is that there are two reasons. First, at sacred times we behave solemnly, seriously, perhaps a bit pompously. To see the cantor enter the sanctuary, bow right, left, and centre, march solemnly to the lectern and then mangle Gregorian chants provided an effect not unlike watching a man walk down the street in the full dignity of bowler hat and furled umbrella slip on a banana skin. The pretensions of his style and the abrupt indignity of its conclusion appeals to the most primal human need to laugh.

Secondly, laughter releases tension. The sacred is awesome, terrible, overwhelming. We are dealing with the cosmic and the Ultimate, the Absolute. If what we are engaged in is anything more than mere thoughtless routine, we are bound to be somewhat tense and frightened. After all, we are contingent and relative and that which is necessary and absolute is something we ought to fear. Thomas More mounting the executioner's scaffold with a jest on his lips, the Irish wake in which death is ridiculed, and the chocolate box circulating among cardinals during Vatican ceremonies all represent ways of reasserting the validity of the commonplace and the ordinary, the human and the earthy, in the face of the extraordinary and the cosmic. Laughter in the most serious of times not only releases tensions, it is also a way the human has of reasserting his own dignity in circumstances in which he may seem the most undignified because he is then the most dependent on forces over which he has no control.

Those who have studied the phenomena of human play have frequently pointed out that the sacred is a form of play, a game, a world set apart from the world of ordinary daily life, with its own rules, its own constraints, its own fantasies. Games can be deadly serious, of course, but because they are serious it does not follow that they are not also playful. Where there is play there is humour. Huizinga, in his famous *Homo Ludens*, asserts that religious ritual is sacred play. Involved in sacred play is the heroic assumption that the deity does not mind in engaging in sport and games with his people. Once that assumption has been made, humour is not only necessary it is also legitimate. We laughed at the vesper cantors because at some level of our personalities we believed that God was laughing too.

One can go further. Where ritual pretends to be sacred and has lost the paradoxical capacity for simultaneously generating reverence and laughter, it has ceased to be very sacred. Some of the "low church" liturgical forms popular in post-conciliar Catholicism are simply not funny. (An outsider may think that a Eucharist produced of Frankfurters and Pepsi Cola or whisky and crackers is bizarre.) Such liturgies have become so commonplace, so ordinary, so everyday, that they are completely out of contact with humankind's experience of the sacred; hence they are no longer capable of engendering laughter. Similarly, some of the glossolalia experiences of the Catholic pentecostal movement (though by no means all of them) have become so commonplace that one feels no impulse to laugh at behaviour which in the objective order would be considered amusing. Indeed, one dare not laugh.

The third kind of religious humour, I call the humour of faith. It was best exemplified for most of us in recent years by Pope John XXIII. It marked the lives of G. K. Chesterton, Philip Neri, St Francis of Assisi. It is the humour rooted in the gaiety and joy that comes from faith, hope, confidence and compassion. One laughs because one knows that no matter how desperate things are they are never serious in the ultimate sense. No matter how long things may go badly they will ultimately end well. No matter how tragic life might appear it is, in the final analysis, a comedy. Such humour is not so much man laughing in the face of death (as occurs at Irish wakes) but rather man laughing at the prospect of life. It is not existential heroism in the face of tragedy; it is existential joy flowing from the conviction that ultimately life is a joke, that God is a comedian, and that the story of our lives will have a happy ending. As Gregory Baum has so neatly put it, "Tomorrow will be different." It is laughter that rocks the walls of hollow tombs. The force of it can roll back stones from those tombs, and the conviction of it assures resurrection.

Such religious humour may be one of the most noble capabilities that humankind has. It is the best guarantee that the humour of ecclesiastical satire will not be required. When churchmen can laugh at themselves—as Pope John did—there will be no opportunities for others to laugh at them. When there is laughter rooted in hope, confidence and compassion, there sardonic laughter will be inappropriate and will no longer find an audience.

But more than that must be said. The sort of contagious joy that flows from the laughter of faith is the best guarantee of effective ecclesiastical ministry that can possibly exist. The matter can be put more strongly. The ecclesiastical minister who is not capable of the laughter of faith stands little if any chance of effective use of his ministry. St Teresa of Avila is alleged to have prayed, "from silly devotions and sour-faced saints, deliver us, O Lord." Why anyone would think that sour-faced saints are more effective ministers than laughing ones is not at all clear; none the less, large numbers of ecclesiastical ministers seem to think that laughter is incompatible with their vocations. It must be confessed that if it is, then so is effectiveness. The clergyman in *Ryan's Daughter* (the only good thing in the film besides the Irish scenery) is one of the most impressive clerics to appear in contemporary literature. A gruff, rough-hewn man, he was very much a product of his own time and place—western Ireland in the first decades of this century. For all his tough, authoritarian style, he was a man of great love and tenderness for his people, and they responded to that love in their own rough way because the ability of priest and people to laugh together in the face of a grim world made them one. He makes an interesting contrast with the clergy in *Roma* and *The Priest's Wife*.

This is an article written in a scholarly journal about ecclesiastical ministers. It begins with a description of a bitter cinematic satire of the failings of such ministers. Yet, if the truth be told, someone could also write an article about the solemn, self-important, pompous seriousness of theologians—and sociologists too, for that matter. It would be singularly inappropriate to conclude this article by saying merely that ecclesiastical ministers should have the courage and faith to be able to laugh at themselves. Theologians and sociologists should do the same thing. Alas, that seems even less likely than laughter ringing through the musty corridors of ecclesiastical institutions. Scholars will begin to laugh at themselves only fifteen minutes after the Parousia.

Marc Tanenbaum

Humour in the Talmud

A FUNDAMENTAL characteristic of humour, Sigmund Freud has written, is that it has in it "a liberating element." That element consists of its "refusal to be hurt by the arrows of reality or to be compelled to suffer. It insists that it is impervious to wounds dealt by the outside world, in fact, that these are merely occasions for affording its pleasure."[1]

By its repudiation of the possibility of suffering, Freud asserts, humour takes its place in the great series of methods devised by the mind of man for evading the compulsion to suffer, which includes self-induced states of abstraction, delusions, and ecstasy. Owing to this connection, humour possesses a dignity which is wholly lacking, for instance, in wit, for the aim of wit is either simply to afford gratification, or in so doing, to provide an outlet for aggressive tendencies. What is fine and elevating about humour is the ego's victorious assertion of its own invulnerability in the face of adverse real circumstances.

The pleasure derived from humour is never so intense as that produced by the comic or by wit and never finds a vent in hearty laughter. Without quite knowing why, we attribute to this less intensive pleasure a high value: we feel it to have a peculiarly liberating and elevating effect. The jest made in humour is not the essential: it has only the value of a demonstration. The principal thing is the intention which humour fulfils, whether it concerns the self or other people. Its meaning is: "Look here.

[1] S. Freud, *Character and Culture* (Essay on "Humour", 1928) (New York, 1963), pp. 265-6.

This is all that this seemingly dangerous world amounts to—
child's play—the very thing to jest about!" Through this mental
device of humour, Freud states, the superego—which is a stern
master—speaks such kindly words of comfort to the intimidated
ego and seeks to protect it from suffering.

Jewish humour expresses quintessentially the psychodynamic
technique by which the Jewish people confronted and endured
the sufferings and horrendous pain inflicted on them by the
anti-Semitism that suffused Western society and culture, both
Christian and secular, for the greater part of almost two thous-
and years of the diaspora. Throughout the diaspora experience,
the Jewish self-image was never wholly independent on the image
the Gentiles had of Jews in either its religious or secular guises.
Nobody escapes unscathed from the role into which the world
has cast him. Most Jews who have incorporated some of the
anti-Semitic attitudes of their environment have found a number
of rational ways of expressing it. The lively and sometimes excessive self-criticism of the Jews may well be seen as an expression
of the originally external Gentile aggression that became internalized as part of the Jewish character.

Although the Bible demonstrates that this self-criticism preceded the diaspora, as Dr Ernest van den Haag observes,[2] the
Jewish superego seems always to have been extraordinarily
powerful—as one might expect in so patriarchal a society—
whether it found expression in prophets or in later social critics
(Marx, Freud, Einstein, Marcuse, et al.). Some highly destructive
Jewish self-criticism bears the earmarks of identification with
the aggressor. Some is expressed in humorous jokes—a harmless
way of discharging aggression.

From biblical and rabbinic times to the present day, the jokes
which Jewish people tell about themselves to themselves are most
frequently about the harshness of the lives they led for many
centuries. Such humour was intended to take the sting out of
suffering—as though suffering itself were funny. It is almost as
if they go out of their way to make jokes about themselves in
order to anticipate the pain the world has in store for them,
and by this anticipation blunt its impact.

[2] E. van den Haag, The Jewish Mystique (New York, 1971), p. 50.

Sholom Aleichem, one of the most famous of all writers in Yiddish, defined hope as "a liar." He said, "April first (Fool's Day) is a joke that is repeated 365 times a year," and "Life is a drama for the wise, a game for the fool, a comedy for the rich, and a tragedy for the poor."

One can almost hear the sigh of acceptance with which these jokes were received when first heard in the wretched ghettos and *shtetls* (villages) of Europe. This is the humour of the deprecating shrug, jokes which rarely make you laugh with the deep roar of pleasure that characterizes much non-Jewish humour. At best, these jokes make you smile for a moment, and that smile is rueful. In effect, Jews make jokes in order not to cry.[3]

This attitude of "moderation" toward humour and its personal and social uses among Jews found theological foundation —or rationalization—in the larger world-view of rabbinic Judaism. The rabbis—who shaped classical Judaism from the period roughly from 100 B.C to A.D. 640 (the date of the completion of the Babylonian Talmud),[4] sought to achieve a balance between life on earth and the life to come (*'ôlām habbôh*). While they perceived this life (*'ôlām hazzeh*) to be full of persecutions and trouble and believed that the next life will be one of felicity and joy, they still thought that a long life on earth was an undoubted blessing, and death, though a prelude to that other life of bliss, was still somehow an evil. They did not abandon this world or cheapen it. Even in this world, the Torah (the Law: not *nomos*, but God's revealed way of life, *paidea*) could be studied and fulfilled, and such study and practice gave indescribable and unique pleasure. In addition, the rabbis were not impervious to other clean and healthy values in mundane pleasures which God has allowed his creatures to enjoy. They could thank him for the beauties of nature. They could enjoy a good dinner. They definitely taught that the pleasures of this world must not and

[3] There are a number of popular works on "Jewish humour", but these are mainly anthologies of anecdotes. Among the better known are: H. Golden, *The Golden Book of Jewish Humour* (New York, 1972); L. Rosten, *Treasury of Jewish Quotations* and *The Joys of Yiddish*; M. Peters, *Wit and Wisdom of the Talmud* (New York, 1940).

[4] J. Neusner, *There We Sat Down; The Story of Classical Judaism* (New York, 1972); *From Politics to Piety: The Emergence of Pharisaic Judaism* (New York, 1973).

should not be despised—so long as they are enjoyed in moderation, sanctified by religion, by gratitude to God, and above all, not allowed to interfere with the study and fulfilment of the Torah, it is wrong to pass them by. It might be necessary to practise some asceticism for the sake of study, then one should do so. But if one can combine the lower with the higher, that is the best manner of life which is possible for the human being. The rabbis were resilient optimists, as C. G. Montefiore[5] called them, and persecution and troubles never daunted their spirits for long.

The rabbis intellectualized and justified the lessons of Jewish history. Whatever befell them, or whatever pain or suffering they underwent themselves, or witnessed in others, two explanations sufficed to maintain their faith. Their own sins, or the sins of their forefathers, merited all the punishment which had come upon them. On the other hand, they held the absolute conviction of the felicities of the future, the world beyond the grave, which would compensate, or more than compensate, for any pains or sufferings in this world. Such compensation would be all the greater and more glorious because of, or in proportion to, these sufferings and pains, and enabled them to withstand unflinchingly any amount of tribulations, and prevented the smallest suggestions or whisperings of doubt. The rabbis would entirely have agreed with Paul when he wrote: "I reckon that the sufferings of the present time are not worthy to be compared with the glory which shall be revealed to us."

The rabbis taught that deliverance must come from God. In the end God will keep his covenant, but meanwhile we must be patient. We must not try to force his hand: we must not fight enemies when our defeat is certain, the supreme lesson learned from the destruction of Jerusalem and the Roman oppression. Instead, they taught that Jews must dedicate themselves to the meticulous fulfilment of his Law, and in addition to being his chosen people, the Jews can remain spiritually superior to their more powerful enemies. They can cultivate their intellects—for this no permission was needed. And they could excel in the activities permitted them. By clinging to this lesson of the rabbis,

[5] C. G. Montefiore and H. Loewe. *A Rabbinic Anthology* (New York, 1938).

the Jews adapted themselves to reality and managed to survive individually and collectively. They managed to keep alive a prideful self-image from which they could draw sustenance and which helped them survive psychically intact. Throughout their history, the Jews were able to keep and to sharpen their identity as "a kingdom of priests and a holy nation," covenanted by the revelation at Mount Sinai to carry out a task of redemption in the world until the coming of the kingdom. They would make major contributions to civilization as soon as they were given an opportunity to do so by the Enlightenment and through the rebirth of the State of Israel.

Apart from the strictly ascetic view by which later medievalists condemned humour and laughter, the rabbis of the Talmudic period saw no reason for such a general condemnation, in so far as humour and laughter express joy and relaxation, quite legitimate "this-worldly" pleasures.

Since to the rabbis all their religion was contained in the Scriptures and they never expressed any view, or enunciated any doctrine which they did not seek to justify or substantiate by some biblical passage or utterance, their views toward humour and its expression in laughter were unusually grounded in biblical sources. Dr Chaim Reines[6] identifies several categories of laughter in biblical and rabbinic literature which reflect the various mental states of relief, joy, embarrassment or play which are accompanied by laughter:

1. *The Laughter of Joy*

In Psalms (126. 2), it is said that when the Lord will return the exultants of Zion "our mouth will be full of laughter and our tongue of song." Laughter and song are, thus, the expression of joy. Laughter is here probably mentioned because the deliverance from exile came so suddenly that it seemed like a dream with its consequent pleasurable relief.

2. *The Laughter of Intellectual Enjoyment*

Laughter, which generally expresses pleasure, occurs at an easy, playful engagement of the intellect. One haggadic passage

[6] C. W. Reines, "Laughter in Biblical and Rabbinic Literature," *Judaism Magazine*, 82, 21, 2 (New York, 1972), pp. 176-83.

(*Tanhuma*, ed. Buber, *Yitro 17: Pesiḳta Rabbati*, ed. Friedman, p. 101) notes the difference in the expression on the face when teaching Bible or Mishnah or delivering an haggadic sermon. In teaching the Bible in the elementary school, the teacher displays a stern face in order to inspire awe before the word of the Lord and, also, respect for his person. In teaching Mishnah and Talmud, the teacher displays a friendly but serious face, since this subject requires considerable mental strain. But when delivering an aggadic sermon before the assembly of laymen the speaker displays a smiling face because the material of the haggadah is not of such a serious character as the *halaḳhah* (religious law) and is based, to a considerable extent, on word plays and similar homiletic devices, and generally gives free rein to the imagination. In fact, the haggadah even sometimes contains witticisms (J. Heinemann, *Darḳhei Haggadah* 190, 191). In order to catch the attention of the audience the speaker sometimes had recourse to audacious statements about some extravagant events, which aroused laughter (Genesis *Rabbah* 30. 9).

3. The Laughter of Confidence

The term laughter (smile) is also used in the Bible to express confidence and the absence of fear in the face of an impending event. (Proverbs 31. 25; Job 5. 22; 39. 22.) A curious story is told in the Talmud (*Makḳot* 24) that Rabbi Akiba, Rabbi Gamliel, Rabbi Joshua, and Rabbi Eliezer once walked in the ruins of the Temple and saw a fox there. While his colleagues broke out in tears at this tragic sight, Rabbi Akiba laughed. When they expressed their astonishment about this inappropriate laughter, Rabbi Akiba (ca. A.D. 135) explained that just as there had been fulfilment of the gloomy forecast of the prophets that the mountain of the Temple would be converted to forest-covered high places (Jeremiah 26. 18; Micah 3. 12; Isaiah 2. 1; Micah 4. 2), so also would there be the fulfilment of the forecast about the future glory of the Temple. The laughter of Rabbi Akiba thus signified his faith in the promises of the prophets in spite of the present plight of the Jewish nation. (A similar story is also found in *Yoma* 38a: *Sheḳalim* 9a.)

4. The Laughter of Sympathy

Laughter (a smile) also signifies friendliness, good will, or intimacy. The rabbis appreciated the ethical meaning of a smile which signifies friendliness, sympathy, consolation. Rabbi Yochanan (ca. A.D. 70) said that a smile is worth more than a gift of milk (Talmud *Ketubot* 111b). By that he meant that what matters is not the material gift, as such, but the showing of sympathy and understanding since an individual in distress needs sympathy and understanding more than anything else. Similarly, it was said (*Baba Batra* 9b) that consoling a poor man with words is worth more than giving him alms.

5. The Laughter of Mocking an Opponent

A frequent cause of laughter (which is ethically reprehensible) is the wish to outwit a hard opponent by using some cunning device, like a legal trick, to defeat him or her. The laughter caused in this case derives from the pleasure taken in the trick used to achieve the victory.

6. The Laughter of Contempt: Derision

Laughter sometimes expresses contempt, since it signifies that the individual arouses only amusement and is not to be feared. Thus in Psalms 2. 4, it is said that the Lord "laughs and mocks" at the kings who plot against him and his messiah. These words means that he scorns them because, in spite of their arrogance, they are really impotent against him. The haggadah also depicts the actual mocking of tyrants. Thus it says that when Moses and Aaron came to Pharaoh to show him, by miracles, the power of the God of Israel, he complained that they were mocking him (meaning scorning him). The haggadah in Exodus *Rabbah* IX, 4, which apparently has in mind the conditions of its time (under Roman Imperial rule) wished to indicate here that the oppressed and persecuted Jews had only scorn for their oppressors, since they were confident they would overcome tyrants. The biblical narrative says that, after the last plague, Pharaoh called Moses and Aaron to tell them that he was prepared to let the Israelites leave the country. The haggadah, wishing to stress Pharaoh's humiliation, presents him as running in panic through the streets and asking the people the whereabouts of Moses and Aaron. The children of the Israelites mocked him and said, "Where are you going, Pharaoh?" (*Tanhumah*, Buber, *Bo* 19).

X ## 7. The Ethics of Laughter

Some kinds of laughter, as mentioned above, are of a malicious nature and must be morally condemned. Besides, excessive laughter hinders the concentration of thought, diverts from the serious tasks of life and leads to frivolity and mischievous pranks. Violent laughter which throws the individual into convulsions (which is found in hysteria) is not in accord with human dignity and is also aesthetically repugnant. Children and primitives laugh constantly and violently, but the civilized person laughs moderately at certain proper occasions and is careful thereby not to offend the feelings of his fellows. These ethical considerations explain the critical attitude to humour and laughter which is apparent in biblical and rabbinic literature.

Ecclesiastes (*Qoheleth*) is the oldest Jewish thinker (apart from some casual references in Proverbs) who devoted attention to laughter from an ethical viewpoint, and his views on the subject show similarity with those of the rabbis. He says, "of laughter I said it is foolish and of merriment what is it for" (2. 2). These words refer to frivolous laughter and merriment which lack any sense. In another place he says that "the laughter of the fools is like the crackling of the thorns under a pot" (7. 6), referring here to the violent and aesthetically repulsive laughter of inferior individuals. He also observed that "better sorrow than laughter for with a sad countenance there is improvement of the mind" (7. 3). Ecclesiastes certainly does not generally recommend sadness, since, quite on the contrary, he recommends joy, but he means that sometimes (as in moral admonition) a sad face is more appropriate than laughter. In another statement he asserts "there is a time for weeping and a time for joy." In accordance with his sound view of life, Ecclesiastes does not repudiate laughter entirely but holds that it should be kept within bounds as the natural expression of joy at proper times and occasions. Excessive laughter is a sign of frivolity and spiritual emptiness.

Rabbi Akiba said that laughter and frivolity lead to licentiousness (*Avot III, 13*). One late midrash says that laughter and
frivolity may lead also to other grave sins, such as murder, de-
ception, and stealing (*Seder Eliahu Rabbah*, ed. Friedman,
ch. XIV, p. 64). The Code of Maimonides, *Deot. VII, 4*, refers
to one who slanders by way of laughter and frivolity.

The rabbis held that the Holy Spirit (*Shekhinah*) rests neither
in a state of sadness nor of laughter and frivolity, but in a state
of joy which is bound with the fulfilment of a *misewah* (meaning, generally, religious devotion) (*Shabbat 30b*). Joy, according
to Maimonides, is the middle way between sadness and frivolity.
One source which describes the way of life which is necessary
for the student of the Torah, states that he should indulge only
in a "minimum of laughter" *meat sehoq*) (*Avot VI, 5*). It should
be noted that this source does not absolutely repudiate laughter
but only excessive laughter.

Rabbi Simon ben Yohai said that in his time (after the destruction of the Temple) one should not indulge in joyous laughter
since it is stated when the Lord delivers Israel our mouth will
be full of laughter. It is apparent from this motivation that
Rabbi Simon ben Yohai did not generally repudiate laughter
as an expression of joy on ascetic grounds but held that it was
not appropriate at the time since one should mourn for Zion.
This view was the result of the tendency which developed then to
forgo excessive joy as a sign of mourning for Zion.

Despite these moral strictures, social historians of the Talmudic period disclose that the ordinary people of the time were
inclined to merriment. There was much merriment and good
humour especially at weddings and at such festivals as Purim
(marking the liberation of Persian Jewry from impending mas-
sacre), and Simchath Torah (the last day of the Festival of Taber-
nacles, Sukkoth, celebrating the divine gift of the Torah). In
fact, even some of the younger rabbinic scholars participated in
such wedding celebrations, although the rigorists among the
rabbis objected. When Rabbi Ashi saw that at the wedding of his
son the young scholars became too merry, he broke a glass in
order to induce them to sobriety (*Berakhot 31a*). The patriarch
Rabbi Judah Hanassi (ca. A.D. 170–210) once declined to invite
Bar Kappara, one of the greatest scholars among his following,

to the wedding of his son because Bar Kappara had the habit of getting merry and speaking jests at weddings.

When Abbaya was once reproached by his teacher, Rabba, for becoming a little merry, he replied, "I am observing the rite of tefillin" (donning the phylactery prayer headpieces and arm-bands), meaning that for a man of his calibre there is no ground for the apprehension that he might become frivolous (*Berakhot 30b*). The haggadah states that Elijah praised two simple men because by their jests and good humour they made sad people merry and succeeded in stopping feuds (*Taanit 22a*).

In sum, although the rabbis of the Talmud denounced "laughter and frivolity," they had a genuine appreciation of the healthy psychological effect of humour and laughter.

PART IV
STATEMENT

Note

This heading replaces the usual "Documentation" section. For want of a generally satisfactory description we have decided on "Statement(s)". It is intended to be a place where—when it seems appropriate and possible—non-theological writers of international reputation can comment on the subject of the particular issue. This is of particular importance for the issues of fundamental theology and borderline questions. It is an attempt to expose each discipline to currents and intellectual attitudes active in today's world, before which Christians have to answer for the hope that is in them. There are also many reasons for thinking that theology can learn much—not least about itself—from such an experiment.

The writers who appear in this section will be asked, not so much for a specialized study from their particular field, but for a general, and always personal, comment. It is in this light that the structure and style of the following contribution by Heinrich Böll should be read.

Heinrich Böll

About Joy

A Statement on the Subject of this Issue

THE representation of joy as something in the future ("You have
sorrow *now*, but you *will* rejoice"), not of the present or to be
expected in the present, has always seemed to me like an attempt
to pass counterfeit coin, in which the gold of hope inside has
been replaced by plaster. It is a permanent inflation, kept up
over centuries, millennia, a thinning and stretching of hope that
turns comfort into empty words. And what makes it more painful is that the empty words come from those who have already
had their comfort and joys on this earth. The "you *will* rejoice"
is always put off into the future or an eternal life, and yet anyone could have worked out or realized that every day, every
hour, has its future. In the first Christian decades and centuries,
even if the bodily return of Christ was expected as an imminent
event, it should not have been necessary for the embodiment
and making present of the God-man at the Lord's Supper to
exclude joy in the present. (The Supper began as a shared meal,
but in the course of centuries was distorted into an abstract
feeding.) The deadly seriousness and joylessness of this ritual
meal carried over into the frightful silence and gloom of bour-
geois meals, the composition of which was dictated almost ex-
clusively by the taste of the master, the master of the house.
Think of all the neurotic children with ruined digestions who
had to eat everything, and eat it all, even if with the most strenu-
ous efforts they could not *like* it. Eating was a duty, not a
pleasure, and the result was nausea to the point of vomiting. We
might well ask who ever enjoyed the taste of a host?

This reduction of a potentially enjoyable family meal to a duty went with another, the reduction of sex to a duty. For women it was turned into the performance of a terrible duty, into a merely tolerated "act", which it was indecent, almost "wanton", to enjoy—illogically, in fact, since most prostitutes have to deny themselves this pleasure. This horrible distortion of sex into a "marital duty" probably results from the mistaken view that sex is only for reproduction, which is again illogical, since it is indisputable from a biological point of view that reproduction without the sexual stimulation and satisfaction of the man is completely impossible. In this concentration on the "content" of sex—reproduction, with its necessary but delicately ignored details—its form was forgotten, and, when one thinks about it, it cannot be only now, it must always have been reflected in society's need for such strangely named people and institutions as "women of pleasure" and "houses of pleasure", people and places by whom and in which mere sexual forms without content could be exchanged. In spite of all that has been said about it, all the complaints and laments, a pretence of misunderstanding seems to lie like a curse over sex. That apart from its content—which, as in art, always comes with it—it can be pleasure as play and both play and pleasure at the same time as form, this is denied. Of course the subject has become so specific to the Church that most people are bored with it, but I still have to mention it in a discussion about joy. The saying, "You have sorrow now, but you will rejoice," must be related to the sexuality of *both* sexes. The example of the child who vomits after a duty meal chosen by others and eaten in silence, a meal which he has not *enjoyed*, can be easily varied: why, for example, do some of the "sexual liberators" and the sexually "liberated" look so haggard?

What has been lacking to date in Christian preaching from all quarters has been tenderness, verbal, erotic and—yes—theological tenderness. (Note: consider the concept of "political tenderness"!)

This hoped-for possibility of a new tenderness in theology and its language excludes the great adversary, which regards joy, humour, irony and imagination, not perhaps as direct obstacles, but certainly as highly suspicious, the Church's system of rules.

There is of course a right to intimacy and tenderness but they cannot be legislated for, and it is and always was both idiotic and criminal to not merely desire, but even require reproduction and at the same time insist on a separation between the form and content of human sexuality, an insistence which, with a conniving wink, pushed pleasure out into the outlying areas of society, where human sex received compassion for payment. There is of course an area for sexual compassion, but here too rules are impossible, obligation lethal and payment murder, if the other side of the "transaction" is meant to be joy. I cannot imagine how many joyless marriages, how many joyless performances of marital duty there may have been, whole continents full of formless or unformed contents. What was painful about *Humanae Vitae* was not its attempt to give people advice on a matter in which they do need advice and comfort; every bishop, the bishop of Rome too, has a right to give advice. What was said about this document was the misrepresentation of sexuality, insisted on again and again, as merely an instrument of reproduction. This misrepresentation conceals a crude materialism. It is precisely because human beings are not merely material beings, or determined by matter, that they need play, forms, fantasy, humour and irony, and to reduce the relation of the sexes to a mere exchange of the "materials" which lead to reproduction is materialism and forces people into a tussle which does not produce salvation, healing or pleasure.

It doesn't take great psychological or psychiatric experience, merely a little imagination, to have some idea of the number of people in whom the joylessness of their sexuality has gone as far as illness—and how many have been cured by pleasure in it, just as many people certainly are made ill by the joylessness of their meals and are cured by a cheerful meal. "You have sorrow now, but you will rejoice." In a man, in a woman, in your husbands and your wives and *with* them! The production of the material joy cannot be controlled by laws, either secular laws or laws of the Church.

Translated by Francis McDonagh

Biographical Notes

GÉRARD BESSIÈRE was born on 27 January 1928 and was ordained priest in 1951. He studied at the Institut Catholique in Paris and at the Sorbonne. He is a licentiate in theology and philosophy. From 1953 until 1963 he ministered to priests and schoolteachers in his diocese (Cahors) and from 1963 until 1969 he was a national chaplain to schoolteachers. Since 1969, he has been working on a thesis, "Jesus in the work of Proudhon", collaborating with the French publisher, Éditions du Cerf, where is is also responsible for the collections, *Terres de Feu* and *Sciences Humaines et Religions*. His own writings include *L'Incognito de Dieu* (Paris, 1970), *Des chrétiens et des mots* (Paris, 1971), *Jésus est devant* (Paris, 1973) and *Le Pape a disparu* (Paris, 1972) and *Le Pape reparaît* (Paris, 1973), a novel, in two volumes, of humour and "Church fiction" (cf. "science fiction"), illustrated by Piem. He is also a member of the editorial committee of the three-monthly review *Jésus,* the first number of which has just appeared.

EUGEN BISER was born in Oberbergen in 1918, studied theology at Freiburg University and became a priest in 1946. He is a doctor of theology and philosophy, consultant to the Secretariat for Non-believers and professor of fundamental theology and director of the Herman-Schell-Institut at Würzburg University. His most notable publications include *Nietzsches Destruktion des christlichen Bewusstseins* (1962); *Theologische Sprachtheorie und Hermeneutik* (1970); *Theologie und Atheismus* (1972); *Der Helfer* (1973).

HEINRICH BÖLL was born on 21 December 1917 in Cologne. He is a freelance author and president of P.E.N. International. He has received several prizes for literature, including the Nobel Prize in 1972. Among his publications are *The Train was on Time* (London, 1956); *Acquainted with the Night* (London, 1955); *The Unguarded House* (London, 1957); *The Clown* (London, 1965); *The End of a Mission* (London, 1968); *Group Portrait with Lady* (London, 1973) and many others.

ERNESTO CARDENAL is a Nicaraguan poet, who was born in that country in 1925. He experienced a deep religious conversion when he was thirty-one and entered a contemplative community, becoming a priest in 1965. Since then, he has founded his own small community, in which he lives on an island in Lake Nicaragua. Among his works translated into English are *Psalms of Struggle and Liberation (Salmos)*; *To Live is to Love (Vida en el Amor)* and *Homage to the American Indians (Homenage a los Indios Americanos)*. Other works include *El Estrecho Dudoso; En Cuba; Canto Nacional; Oraculo sobre Managua* (all published in Buenos Aires).

JACQUES COLETTE was born in 1929 and is a doctor of philosophy and theology. He is also a member of the Kierkegaard Selskab (Copenhagen). His most important works are *The Difficulty of Being Christian* (London, 1968); *Histoire et Absolu* (Paris, 1972); "A Fé segundo Kierkegaard", *Credo para Amanhã* (Petrópolis, 1972). He has also published many studies of contemporary history of philosophy in *La Revue Nouvelle, La Revue des Sciences Philosophiques et Théologiques, Kierkegaardiana, La Revue Philosophique de Louvain, La Revue de Théologie et de Philosophie, Schweizerischer Rundschau, Esprit*, etc.

FRANCIS FIORENZA was born in 1941 in Brooklyn, New York. He received his doctorate in theology from the University of Münster (Germany) for his study *Eschatology and Progress: The Theological Problematic of Ernst Bloch's Philosophy of History*. He is at present assistant professor of systematic theology at the University of Notre Dame. He has published a series of articles on "Dialectical Theology and Hope", I, II and III, *Heythrop Journal* (1968-1969). He has written the introduction to the English translation of Karl Rahner's *Spirit in the World* (London and Sydney, 1968) and has edited a special issue of *Continuum* on "Jürgen Habermas and the Critical Theory of the Frankfurt School" (1970) and has contributed "Der Mensch als Einheit von Leib und Seele" to *Mysterium Salutis*.

ANDREW GREELEY was born in Oak Part, U.S.A. in 1928 and ordained in 1954. He studied in the United States at the Seminary of St Mary of the Lake and at Chicago University. Master of arts, licentiate in theology, doctor of sociology, he is a lecturer in the Department of Sociology at Chicago University and Senior Study Director of the National Opinion Research Center at the same university. Among his published works are *The Hesitant Pilgrim. American Catholicism after the Council* (New York, 1966); *A Future to Hope In* (New York, 1969); *Contemporary Religion* (Glenview, Ill., 1972) and *Priests in the United States. Reflections on a Survey* (New York, 1972).

MICHAEL LANDMANN was born on 16 December 1913 in Basle (Switzerland), studied philosophy and psychology in Basle and Paris and gained his doctorate in 1939. Since 1951 he has been a professor at the Free University of Berlin, specializing in ancient philosophy. His works include *Ursprungs-bild und Schöpfertat—zum platonisch-biblischen Gespräch* (1966). Most of his other books are concerned with philosophical anthropology; see,

158   BIOGRAPHICAL NOTES

for example, *"De homine"*. *Eine Geschichte der Philosophischen Anthropologie* (1962) and *Das Ende des Individuums* (1971).

NORBERT SCHIFFERS, born 14 July 1927 in Aachen, became a priest in 1952. He studied at Tübingen University, where he gained his doctorate in 1954 and qualified to teach theology in 1966. He is at present professor in fundamental theology at Regensburg University. Among other works, he has published *Einheit der Kirche* (Düsseldorf, 1956); *Fragen der Physik an die Theologie* (Düsseldorf, 1968); *Befreiung zur Freiheit* (Regensburg, 1971); *Zur Theorie der Religion* (Freiburg, 1973).

DOROTHEE SÖLLE, who is a doctor of philosophy, was born in 1929. She studied theology, philosophy and literature in Cologne, Freiburg and Göttingen. Her books include *Christ the Representative* (London, 1967); *The Truth is Concrete* (London and New York, 1969); *Atheistisch an Gott glauben* (Olten, 1968); *Phantasie und Gehorsam* (Stuttgart, 1968); *Das Recht, ein anderer zu werden* (Neuwied, 1971); *Realisation. Studien zum Verhältnis von Theologie und Dichtung nach der Aufklärung* (Neuwied, 1973); *Themen der Theologie* (Stuttgart, 1973).

DAVID STEERE, born in 1931 in Akron. Ohio, studied at the Louisville Presbyterian Theological Seminary, B.D. 1956, and at the Union Theological Seminary, New York, TH.D., 1966. Since 1966 he has been professor of Pastoral Theology and director of Field Education, Louisville Presbyterian Theological Seminary. Among his publications are "The DEEP Experience", *Explorations in Ministry*, G. Douglass Lewis, ed. (1971); *The Bodily Expression of the Ego States* (1972). He has also contributed articles to many reviews such as *Psychology Today, Presbyterian Survey* and *Journal of Pastoral Care*.

FULBERT STEFFENSKY is a doctor of theology and was born in 1933. He studied theology at Maria Laach, Beuron and Bochum. He teaches educational theory and practice at the Institute of Education in Cologne. With Dorothee Sölle, he has published *Politisches Nachtgebet in Köln* (I, 1969; II, 1970). In addition to numerous articles in journals, he has also written *Gott und Mensch—Herr und Knecht? Autoritäre Religion und menschliche Befreiung im Religionsbuch* (Hamburg, 1973).

MARC TANENBAUM was born in Baltimore in 1925 and is a rabbi. He studied at the Jewish Theological Seminary of America, at the Johns Hopkins University in Baltimore and at Yeshiva University in New York. He is national director of the ecumenical and interdenominational programme of the American Jewish Committee in New York. An international authority on Jewish-Christian relations, Rabbi Tanenbaum serves as co-secretary of a joint Jewish liaison committee with the Vatican and the World Council of Churches. His publications include *A Guide to Jewish Traditions and Holy Days. Jewish-Christian Dialogue* (1966) and *Our Moral and Spiritual Resources for International Cooperation*.